HOW TO GET WHAT YOU PRAY FOR

How to Get What You Pray For

Harmonizing Your Desires with God's

by BILL AUSTIN

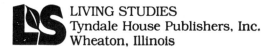
LIVING STUDIES
Tyndale House Publishers, Inc.
Wheaton, Illinois

Scripture quotations, unless otherwise indicated, are from the King James Version of the Bible. Other Scripture quotations are from the *New American Standard Bible* (NASB), © The Lockman Foundation, 1960, 1962, 1963, 1968, 1971; *The New English Bible* (NEB), © 1976 by Oxford University Press, Inc.; *The Holy Bible, New International Version* (NIV), © 1978 by New York International Bible Society; *The New Testament in Modern English*, J. B. Phillips (PHIL), © 1958, 1959, 1972; *The Holy Bible: Revised Standard Version* (RSV), © 1952 by Division of Christian Education of the National Council of Churches of Christ in the United States; *The Living Bible* (TLB), © 1971 by Tyndale House Publishers; and *The New Testament in the Language of the People*, Charles B. Williams (WMS), © 1966 by Edith H. Williams.

First printing, February 1984
Library of Congress Catalog Card Number 83-50970
ISBN 0-8423-1473-3
Copyright © 1984 by Bill R. Austin
All rights reserved
Printed in the United States of America

CONTENTS

Introduction: The Principle of Harmony 7

Part 1   Prayers in Harmony with Each Other   11
1. Primary Prayer: What Do You Want?   15
2. Secondary Prayer: How Do You Want It Done?   27
3. Motive Prayer: Why Do You Want It?   39

Part 2   Pray in Harmony with God   51
4. In His Power: The Heavenly Father   55
5. In His Name: The Human Son   65
6. In His Will: The Holy Spirit   73

Part 3   Pray in Harmony with Yourself   83
7. As the Image of God   87
8. As the Child of God   93
9. As the Handiwork of God   101

Part 4   Pray in Harmony with Nature   109
10. An Orderly World   113
11. A Benevolent World   121
12. A Redemptive World   129

Part 5   Answers in Harmony with Christ's Words   137
13. Everyone Who Asks Receives   143
14. He Who Seeks Finds   153
15. To Him Who Knocks It Will Be Opened   163

INTRODUCTION
THE PRINCIPLE OF HARMONY

Have you received everything you ever prayed for? Of course not. No one has. And no thoughtful person would want to live in a world where every wish of every individual is granted. Many of our prayers are childish, selfish, unwise, and in conflict with our best interests, and sometimes in conflict with the needs and the welfare of others. You know that chaos would erupt if God suddenly gave everybody on earth exactly what they are praying for today.

But, while no one really expects a wise heavenly Father to give every child everything he asks for, the Bible does contain some strong promises along that very line. Jesus said, "Ask, and it shall be given you" (Matt. 7:7). He also promised: "What things soever ye desire, when ye pray, believe that ye receive them, and ye shall have them" (Mark 11:24). Concerning corporate prayer he said, "If two of you shall agree on earth as touching any thing that they shall ask, it shall be done for them of my Father which is in heaven" (Matt. 8:19). He also said, "If ye abide in me, and my words abide in you, ye shall ask what ye will, and it shall be done unto you" (John 15:7).

What are we to make of these promises of Christ in view of the fact that many of our prayers appear to be unanswered? Since prayer is at the very heart of our relationship to God, we should be deeply concerned to know what

Christ meant in his prayer promises, and why we often don't get what we pray for.

I believe that Jesus meant every promise that he made, and that God has the intention and the power to fulfill those promises. However, and this is the most important "however" in this book, Jesus was not telling us how to manipulate or change God. He was telling us how to get ourselves in harmony with God's purpose and plan.

The key word in that last sentence is the word *harmony*. God himself is complete harmony. There is no discord or disunity in the Godhead. God's original creation was harmonious. He created a *universe*, not a *multiverse*. Natural disasters are the result of some elements being out of harmony with each other. Moral disasters are the result of men being out of harmony with each other and with God. Prayer disasters, unanswered or unsuccessful prayers, are the result of man's desires being out of harmony with God's designs.

The first step in learning how to get what you pray for is to understand what prayer *is* and what it *is not*. Prayer is not convincing God to do something for you which he has never thought of nor wants to do. Prayer is getting yourself in harmony with the plans which God has for you, which he wants to fulfill in your life.

The second step in learning how to get what you pray for is to be willing to change your method or style of praying if you realize that you have not been praying in harmony with the dynamic principles of the prayer process.

Most Christians never change their prayer style. They keep praying for the same kind of things in about the same way all their lives. Their record of success in getting what they pray for remains about the same. They grow to expect a certain number of answers or they become cynical about the whole business of praying.

You don't have to keep getting the same kind of results year after year. Your success percentage in praying can be drastically increased. Once you are in harmony with the essential agents of prayer, you will begin to see that the promises of Christ are very real, that you can actually get what you pray for.

The Principle of Harmony

The first major section of this book is titled "Prayers in Harmony with Each Other." You do not have just one prayer going at a time. You have many prayers in various stages of being prayed and being answered. You need to understand the importance of all your prayers being in harmony with each other.

The last major section of the book is titled "Answers in Harmony with Christ's Words." The very reason that we have any hope of answered prayer rests in the biblical promises, especially in the words of Jesus Christ. It is reasonable, then, that we expect only answers which are in harmony with his teachings.

Does this mean that praying prayers that are in harmony with each other will produce answers that are in harmony with Christ's words? Not yet. There are other principles which must be engaged before the harmonious prayers and harmonious answers are united.

You must pray in harmony with the nature of God as he is revealed in Holy Scripture. You must pray in harmony with your own basic nature as you relate to God. You must pray in harmony with the reality of nature in God's created world.

These three agents—God, Self, and Nature—form a bridge between your prayers and their answers. Below is an abbreviated version of the table of contents to show at a glance the relationship of each of these parts as you begin to employ the principle of harmony in your prayer life.

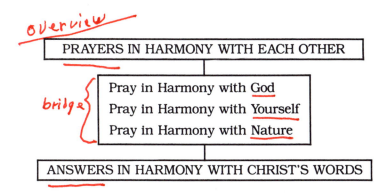

PART 1

Prayers in Harmony with Each Other

"While with an eye
made quiet by the power
Of harmony,
and the deep power of joy,
We see into the life of things."

WILLIAM WORDSWORTH
Above Tintern Abbey

ALL PRAYERS are not the same. In any given day you may pray several kinds of prayers, such as confession, praise, thanksgiving, intercession, or petition. Each type of prayer has a special character of its own, yet no prayer should be out of character with the other types of prayer which you express. If you were praying audibly anyone should be able to recognize that this prayer, regardless of which type it is, is consistent with your basic character and is in harmony with the other kinds of prayer you pray.

Also, each prayer within a given category should be in harmony with your other prayers in that same category. In order to evaluate the presence or absence of harmony in the various categories of my prayer life I try to identify my prayers as either *primary* prayers or *secondary* prayers, a practice I want to help you learn to do.

A primary prayer represents your real desire. A secondary prayer represents your idea of how to bring about the fulfillment of that desire. Ideally, the two should be in harmony, both as to concept and order of importance. If I see that a secondary prayer is not in harmony with my primary prayer, I understand why it cannot be granted. Also, if I allow a secondary prayer to become a primary prayer, my whole prayer life loses its sense of direction and harmony.

Prayers in Harmony with Each Other

Think of primary prayer as seeking God to help you achieve the *general goals* of your life and secondary prayers as the *specific items* which help to arrive at those goals. There will be many more secondary prayers than primary. Any one primary prayer may have dozens or hundreds of related secondary prayers.

The important thing to grasp right now is the fact that your prayers are related to each other. They are not isolated requests which may or may not be answered. They are intertwining concerns and requests which affect each other. It is absolutely imperative, therefore, that your prayers in any category are in harmony with each other and in harmony with the spirit of the other categories.

Before an orchestra begins to play, the musicians tune their instruments. Each instrument must be in tune with itself, and all the instruments must be tuned in to the same lead instrument of the concertmaster. The bedlam caused by the tuning process is an irritating noise to the waiting audience. Yet, it is necessary for the later pleasure of symphonic harmony.

Our early efforts to get our prayers more in tune with our beloved Concertmaster may at first produce confusing noise, but as we stay together and tune one instrument after another, we will be rewarded with the harmony of a more integrated and successful prayer life.

CHAPTER ONE
PRIMARY PRAYER:
What Do You Want?

"Prayer is the soul's sincere desire,
Uttered or unexpressed;
The motion of a hidden fire,
That trembles in the breast."

JAMES MONTGOMERY, *What Is Prayer?*

You may feel that you are not a very strong Christian because so many of your prayer requests have not been granted. I think it is very possible that you are more successful at praying than you realize. You may have been counting the failures of your secondary prayers, and overlooking the persistent, long-range life of your primary prayers.

If you think that your faith must be weak because you keep getting "rejection slips," start concentrating on the general principle instead of the specific items. We will talk about secondary prayers, the specific items, later but right now let us focus on the primary prayers of your soul. I honestly believe you will receive a fresh new second wind of faith when you realize that God may not have given a final answer after all, that he is still working on your primary prayers.

I have developed some simple guidelines which help me to determine which of my prayers are primary. I think these will also help you to get your prayers into harmony with each other.

PRIMARY PRAYER COMES FROM YOUR TOTAL SELF

James Montgomery says that "Prayer is the soul's sincere desire." This is especially true of what I call primary prayer. In biblical usage the term "soul" referred to the total person, both physical and spiritual.

Biblical writers also spoke of the very essence of man as his heart. A special prayer promise in Psalm 37:4 is: "Delight thyself also in the Lord; and he shall give thee the desires of thine heart." The word "heart" here means the total substance of your life, your innermost being, the core of your basic nature. Primary prayer originates in and faithfully represents the very essence of your being. It is the bottom-line desire of your life.

The word "desire" is also important for identifying and understanding primary prayer. We have already noted that the psalmist promised that God will give you "the desires of your heart." Jesus echoed that promise: "What things soever ye desire, when ye pray, believe that ye receive them, and ye shall have them" (Mark 11:24).

"Desire," in the biblical promises, does not mean a superficial wish, a momentary whim, or a carnal fancy. It does not mean that you can have whatever you happen to want whenever you want it. Don't let the common usage of the word "desire" lead you to think that God is obligated to give you anything for which you have an attraction or appetite. The desires of primary prayer are those things which you seek and crave in your subconscious self. God does not promise to give you whims of the moment but desires of the heart. You must learn to distinguish between the momentary wishes and the primary desires in order to understand the kind of prayer answers you have been getting.

One of the most famous examples of the relationship between primary and secondary prayer is given in the

Confessions of Augustine, the great theologian of the fifth century. As a young man, Augustine was quite a libertine, living a loose life which caused his mother, Monica, great anxiety. She prayed constantly for her son that he would be brought to God and dedicate his great mind to the cause of Christ. One day Augustine told Monica that he was going to leave their home on the north coast of Africa and go to Rome to study philosophy. Monica was completely distraught. Rome was then the center of every form of licentiousness, and she knew exposure to all that wickedness would surely destroy her restless, brilliant son. She prayed earnestly that he would not go, she pleaded with both her son and God to stop those foolish plans. Both seemed to turn a deaf ear to her. The headstrong young Augustine sailed for Italy, leaving behind a brokenhearted mother, whose prayer had evidently been unanswered.

Then, a strange chain of events began to happen. In Italy Augustine came under the influence of Ambrose, the eloquent and brilliant young bishop of Milan. After a dramatic conversion experience, Augustine dedicated his life to Christ and became one of the truly great theologians of the early church.

In one of his prayers in the *Confessions*, Augustine refers to his mother's "unanswered" prayer concerning his going to Italy: "Thou in the depths of thy counsels, hearing the main point of her desire, regardest not what she then asked, that thou mightest make me what she ever desired." Monica's primary prayer was that God's will be done in her son's life. Her secondary prayer, telling God how to accomplish the primary request, was for God to keep him away from Italy. But, God knew that he had, prepared and waiting in Italy, the very instrument to bring about the answers to Monica's primary prayer.

So, lift up your head! Don't be so downcast and disappointed that God hasn't answered your most recent secondary prayer. He has not forgotten the deep yearning of your soul, your sincere primary prayer which represents the real you.

PRIMARY PRAYER CONFORMS TO BIBLICAL STANDARDS

The second guideline for identifying the primary prayer of a Christian is its faithfulness to the principles of the Bible. It is not enough to just say that primary prayer represents your total being, your true self, and your heart's desire. Even unbelievers and unspiritual church members have sincere desires of the soul. There are other tests for the primary prayer which Christians can expect God to honor, and conforming to biblical standards is one of the most vital tests.

The ultimate criterion, or measure, for every Christian teaching is the inspired Word of God. This criterion applies to anything we believe or teach about prayer. Any philosophy or testimony we have about prayer must conform to the biblical pattern. Regardless of how sincere we are or how convincing the "evidence" may seem, if our witness about prayer contradicts the biblical message, it is not an authentic Christian witness.

Regardless of how deep your desire lies within you, even if it is the consuming passion of your life, it is not a primary prayer which God will honor unless it can be supported by his Word. Let us suppose that someone has wronged you, and you feel that it is only right for that person to be exposed and punished. The desire to get even becomes a major drive for you. Every day you see and hear things that remind you of the injustice you have suffered. You begin to imagine ways in which the guilty party can be made to pay for your hurt. You may never actually pray for God to do such and such to your enemy, but your desires and designs in that direction really amount to a primary concern, thus, a primary prayer. Your secondary prayers, the specific ways in which that person can be punished, may all harmonize with your primary goal to get even.

But, none of this can be a legitimate Christian attitude, goal, or prayer. The Bible is very plain and explicit about not seeking vengeance and about forgiving our enemies. (See Exod. 23:4; Prov. 24:17; Prov. 25:21; Matt. 5:44; Rom. 12:17-21; Lev. 19:18; Prov. 20:22; Prov. 24:29; Matt. 5:39; 1 Thess. 5:15.) A simple test would be to open the Bible to each of these passages, read the passage over at least three times, then place your finger on that passage as you try to pray your prayer of vengeance for God to strike down your enemy. You cannot do it. A Christian simply cannot succeed in making the consuming desire of his heart something in contradiction to God's holy Word. Your primary prayer absolutely must be in harmony with the spirit and teachings of the Scriptures.

PRIMARY PRAYER WANTS WHAT GOD WANTS

The success of all praying is directly connected to the relationship between the heavenly Father and his children. Look at Psalm 37:4 again: "Delight thyself also in the Lord, and he shall give thee the desires of thine heart." A loose, but rather accurate paraphrase of this verse could read, "When you want what God wants, then you can have what you want."

You may be thinking, "I knew there was a catch to it. I can get what I pray for only if it's something God wants me to have." But, wait a minute! Should a Christian want anything that God does not want? Could we even be happy with anything else?

Our God is a loving, heavenly Father who wants to give us only what is best for us. "Every good gift and every perfect gift is from above, and cometh down from the Father of lights, with whom is no variableness, neither shadow of turning" (James 1:17).

Remember, prayer is getting yourself in harmony with the plans God has for you, which he wants to fulfill in your life. It is the exciting discovery of the gifts God has waiting for you.

Some of God's gifts are spiritual and some are material. Look at these samples of spiritual gifts: "I will give them an everlasting name, that shall not be cut off" (Isa. 56:5). "I will give them an heart to know me" (Jer. 24:7). "I will give them one heart, and I will put a new spirit within you; and I will take the stony heart out of their flesh, and will give them a heart of flesh" (Ezek. 11:19). "Come unto me, all ye that labour and are heavy laden, and I will give you rest" (Matt. 11:28). "If ye then, being evil, know how to give good gifts unto your children: how much more shall your heavenly Father give the Holy Spirit to them that ask him?" (Luke 11:13). "I give unto them eternal life, and they shall never perish" (John 10:28). "Be thou faithful unto death, and I will give thee a crown of life" (Rev. 2:10).

God is also interested in our physical needs, and the Bible gives some samples of his material gifts: "And God said, Behold, I have given you every herb bearing seed, and every tree" (Gen. 1:29). "It is [God] that giveth thee power to get wealth" (Deut. 8:18). "I will give you the rain of your land . . . that thou mayest gather in thy corn, and thy wine, and thine oil" (Deut. 11:14). "He giveth his beloved sleep" (Ps. 127:2). "[He] giveth food to all flesh" (Ps. 136:25).

Don't be afraid of wanting only what God wants. He will not rob you of anything good and needful. On the contrary, wanting what he wants opens up possibilities even you had not imagined. "Eye hath not seen, nor ear heard, neither have entered into the heart of man, the things which God hath prepared for them that love him" (1 Cor. 2:9).

Wanting what God wants must mean an honest willingness to abandon our plans if they are not in harmony with God's. We must be sure that we are not merely projecting our desires into a manufactured image of God.

In the *Devils of Loudun*, Aldous Huxley said of the Abbe Grandier: "A long religious training had not abolished or even mitigated his self-love; it had served only to provide the ego with a theological alibi. The untutored egotist merely wants what he wants. Give him a theological education, and it becomes obvious to him, it becomes axiomatic, that what *he* wants is what God wants."

So, you see, there can be great danger in praying for only what God wants if, in fact, we intend to use such a prayer to get what we want.

In Maxwell Anderson's *Anne of the Thousand Days*, Henry the Eighth said to Thomas Boleyn, "God answers prayer. That's known. Every morning I go on my knees and pray that what I do may be God's will. I pray to him to direct me, that whatever thought comes to my mind, whatever motion floods in my heart, shall be God's will, and I only his instrument." Boleyn wisely replied, "This is a noble thought, of course, but your Majesty realizes that it might be used as an excuse for doing as you please."

How can you avoid that danger? How can you be sure that your idea of what God wants is not your own selfish desire? You must come back again to the Bible. A consistent life-style of mature and successful praying is simply not possible without a working knowledge of the Scriptures. To get what you want through prayer, you must want what God wants. To know what God wants you must know God. To know God you must diligently study his Word. "Then shall we know, if we follow on to know the Lord" (Hosea 6:3).

PRIMARY PRAYER INCLUDES PERSONAL INVOLVEMENT

Your "soul's sincere desire" becomes a primary prayer when you are willing to be personally involved in the fulfillment of that request. Plainly stated, are you willing to be an answer to your own prayer?

Although a primary prayer must conform to the Bible and must be what God wants, it does not become your own personal spiritual yearning unless you are ready to be used in making the dream come true. Primary prayer does not ask merely that God will do something but that you are willing for him to do it through you.

Francis of Assisi did not just pray for world peace; he prayed:

> Lord,
>   make me an instrument of Your peace.
>   Where there is hatred let me sow love;
>   Where there is injury, pardon;
>   Where there is doubt, faith;
>   Where there is despair, hope;
>   Where there is darkness, light; and
>   Where there is sadness, joy.

> O divine Master,
>   Grant that I may not so much
>   Seek to be consoled as to console;
>   To be understood as to understand;
>   To be loved as to love;
>   For it is in giving that we receive;
>   It is in pardoning that we are pardoned; and
>   It is in dying that we are born to eternal life.

Even a basic Christian principle does not constitute a genuine primary prayer until you are committed to living out that principle. For example, in Christian compassion you may pray that God will remove poverty and its accompanying suffering from the earth.

That sounds pretty basic (primary) to Christian love, but the Bible doesn't give any basis to hope that that kind of umbrella prayer will be suddenly and miraculously answered. In fact, Jesus said we will always have the poor with us (Matt. 26:11). But, he also taught that we should give of our own possessions in order to help the poor (Matt. 19:21). Paul said that we should remember the poor (Gal. 2:10) and be ready to share our goods with those who have less (1 Tim. 6:17-18).

Thus, a scriptural primary prayer would be for God to show you how you can live with less and share so that others will not suffer. The larger prayer for God to remove all poverty from the earth may make you feel compassionate and benevolent, but you will never see that prayer answered. On the other hand, if you sincerely pray about your personal responsibility and are willing to respond to specific needs around you, you will receive a clear answer and probably rather quickly.

What have you been praying for in recent years that is serious enough and basic enough to constitute a primary prayer? Peace? Revival? Conversion of the lost? Missions? Wisdom? Unity in the church? Reconciliation of enemies? Relief of the oppressed? Guidance for others? Happiness for some who are lonely, unloved, depressed, scared?

These are marvelous subjects for prayer, and should become so ingrained in your concern that they become true primary prayers. But they can't and won't until you are actually willing to do something to bring about the answer yourself. I don't know what or how much God will want you to do. I just know it is not a serious, primary prayer unless you are volunteering to help at the same time you are crying out to God for help.

PRIMARY PRAYER ACCEPTS CONSEQUENCES

Primary prayer is what you truly want because it is what God wants, regardless of what it costs you. Every answered prayer brings a change of some kind into your life. Things are never the same after God begins to work. Are you sure you are willing to accept the consequences of your deep primary prayer?

The most spiritual and unselfish prayers may produce the most frightening chain reaction. In one of my former pastorates, a very sincere and humble woman rededicated her life one Sunday evening and told me that she wanted more faith. She was really burdened about it, insisting that the greatest lack in her spiritual life was a strong and sufficient faith to weather all storms. I cautioned her that such a prayer might bring severe testing because the only way God could give her more faith was to place her in a position where she needed more. She, nevertheless, insisted that she wanted me to pray with her for a stronger faith.

The very next evening she and her husband came to our home, absolutely frantic because their sixteen-year-old son had not come home from school and seemed to have vanished from our small town. As we knelt in our living room to pray, she said, "Now I know what you meant last night about God giving more faith by giving you the need for more."

Ten days later, the boy returned home from a disappointing trip to California, which he had thought would be a glamorous adventure. I don't know how much he learned from his little escapade, but I saw his mother's faith mature and blossom as she proved herself adequate to face the consequences of her prayer for more faith.

The title of this book may have caused you to envision a wide-eyed child on Christmas Eve getting everything he had wished for, totally free, with no strings attached. This is the vision that many people want to transform into reality where prayer is concerned. But, nothing could be farther from the truth about real primary prayer.

It is true that salvation is the free gift of God (Eph. 2:8) as is eternal life (Rom. 6:23). Yet, here in this earthly life we receive those things which are the result of our joint venture with God, "for we are labourers together with God" (1 Cor. 3:9). Every answered prayer has a price tag which we must be willing to pay.

In another of my former pastorates, a fine young man came to see me about his desire to be a minister. He really felt "called" and was disappointed that his prayers for involvement in the ministry were going unheeded. I asked him if he really knew what he was praying for. I explained to him some of the responsibilities and difficulties of the ministry. I outlined the long educational training ahead for him and described the process of eventually becoming a pastor.

He immediately began to cool off in his ardor for a long-range program. He insisted, however, that he still felt called to preach and believed that God could and would use him. I also believe that God can and sometimes does use preachers without advanced education, so I assured him that I would pray with him about his desire to preach.

Within a few weeks he was asked to fill the pulpit for a friend in a small church. He was overwhelmed by the feeling of responsibility and inadequacy. After getting his opportunity to preach he was more than satisfied to return to his regular job. His humble attitude was, "I didn't really know what I was praying for." He wanted to preach, but he did not want all the work and responsibility that go along with preaching. He started out saying, "I want to preach more than anything," which sounds like a primary desire, but it was a desire without commitment. Every primary prayer carries with it a commitment to accept the consequences of the answer.

Willingness to accept consequences does not of itself

constitute a biblical primary prayer. You may be perfectly willing and able to accept the consequences of payments and maintenance on a new home you are praying for, but does God want you to have the home in the first place? He may have other plans for you and your money. He may know someone else who needs that particular home more than you do.

So, all the various aspects of primary prayer need to interact and harmonize with each other. Look at them again.

Primary prayer comes from your total self.

Primary prayer conforms to biblical standards.

Primary prayer wants what God wants.

Primary prayer includes involvement.

Primary prayer accepts consequences.

When you begin to learn and practice these principles of primary prayer, you will begin to notice that you are getting what you are persistently and patiently praying for on a strong biblical foundation.

If you are still not sure about the presence and position of primary prayer in your relation to God, it should become clearer in the next chapter, which deals with the specific requests of secondary prayer and how they relate to the essence of primary prayer.

CHAPTER TWO
SECONDARY PRAYER:
How Do You Want It Done?

"We, ignorant of ourselves,
Beg often our own harms, which the wise powers
Deny us for our good; so find we profit
By losing of our prayers."

WILLIAM SHAKESPEARE, *Anthony and Cleopatra*

Most of our "unanswered" prayers are what I call secondary prayers. In the primary prayer, we tell God *what* the deep desire of our soul is. In the secondary prayer, we try to tell God *how* to fulfill the desire. God honors and answers, in his wisdom and time, the primary prayer which meets the guidelines we discussed in the previous chapter. Sometimes he also honors and answers our secondary prayers. Many times he does not. Our attitude and reaction about an unanswered secondary prayer reveals how sincere we are about our primary prayer.

SECONDARY PRAYERS MAY BE UNNECESSARY

Paul wrote about an unanswered prayer in his life. "And lest I should be exalted above measure through the abundance of the revelations, there was given to me a thorn in the flesh. . . . for this thing I besought the Lord thrice, that it might depart from me" (2 Cor. 12:7, 8).

This urgent plea of the apostle was answered by God's beautiful assurance, "My grace is sufficient for thee, for my strength is made perfect in weakness" (2 Cor. 12:9). But, as beautiful and assuring as those words are, that is not what Paul prayed for. He prayed specifically that the "thorn in the flesh" would be removed, not for sufficient grace. Was his prayer unanswered? Had he prayed wrongly, or not in accordance with God's will?

This was a secondary prayer, which was very understandable but not necessary for the fulfilling of Paul's primary goals and primary prayer. Paul's great reason for being was for Christ to live in and through him (Phil. 1:21; Gal. 2:20). His primary desire was to be used for the proclamation of the gospel. He asked the Thessalonians to "pray for [him], that the word of the Lord may have free course, and be glorified" (2 Thess. 3:1). That was his primary prayer which he prayed for himself and which he asked others to pray for him.

When he was stricken with the "thorn in the flesh," he obviously felt that it would impede his ministry or keep Christ from living victoriously in and through him. Naturally, he was human, and would have liked to be rid of the pain and inconvenience brought on by the "thorn." The desire for relief, however, was never as strong as the desire to glorify Christ and preach his gospel at any cost.

I think God was actively continuing to answer Paul's primary prayer (to glorify Christ) and then proceeded to explain to him that turning down the secondary request could actually enhance and strengthen Paul's primary reason for living. Paul's response practically declared this to be the case: "Most gladly therefore will I rather glory in my infirmities, that the power of Christ may rest upon me. Therefore, I take pleasure in infirmities, in reproaches, in necessities, in persecutions, in distresses, for Christ's sake: for when I am weak, then am I strong" (2 Cor. 12:9, 10).

Paul was given new insight and new strength which would better enable him to fulfill his primary purpose in life. His contemporaries, both friends and enemies, were closely watching his life, and how he handled his "thorn in the flesh" testified to the authenticity of his faith. Then, for two thousand years his words on the subject have comforted and encouraged literally millions of Christians who have had to face the bewildering questions of injustice and suffering. The world would be poorer, indeed, if the magnificent words of 2 Corinthians 12:7-10 had never been written, as they would not if the "thorn" had been removed.

No, I don't think Paul prayed wrongly, because he quickly saw the message involved and the necessity of the situation, and used it to strengthen both his faith and his testimony. His prayer would have been wrong if it had been the very ground of his faith and the reason for being. If he had said, "This physical infirmity must be healed or I cannot believe in or serve God," that would have been a very primary, but very wrong prayer.

SECONDARY PRAYERS ARE NOT THE FOUNDATION OF OUR FAITH

A secondary prayer may or may not be granted, depending on whether God chooses it to facilitate the biblical primary prayer. A mature Christian does not have his faith shattered when God chooses to work through something other than his secondary prayer. Neither does a mature Christian use an answered secondary prayer to prove that his faith is authentic or that Christianity itself is valid.

My wife and I feel that the house we now own was a very definite answer to prayer. It is located and arranged perfectly for our needs. The financing arrangement was also exactly what we had to have to make this move. God obviously chose to use this secondary prayer to help promote the fulfillment of our primary prayer, to be in the right place doing the right thing for him. However, as nice as this development has been, getting this particular house, even on the terms we set, does not validate our religion. God did that on Easter morning when he raised

Christ from the dead. My faith is not based on what God does about my housing needs but what he did through his Son.

Primary prayer expresses our deepest heart's desire according to God's nature as revealed to us in his Word. Secondary prayer expresses to God our idea or our preference as to how that primary prayer can best be accomplished.

Sometimes we are right on target and our secondary prayer harmonizes with God's plan and we are privileged to receive an affirmative answer to both the secondary and primary request. Often, however, our first secondary prayer must be waived, until through the process of elimination we discover the "how" that harmonizes with the "what."

It was all right and understandable for Monica to pray for Augustine to stay home, because her fears were real, but her knowledge was limited. We should not feel guilty or even hesitant about praying secondary prayers, but we must remember that God knows things that we don't know, and we must keep praying the primary prayer even if our human idea for accomplishing it appears to be wrong.

SECONDARY PRAYERS SHOULDN'T TRY TO PRESSURE GOD

If God takes too long to answer our prayer, we are prone to get impatient and to take matters in our own hands. We may even use our prayers as the means of putting things back in our control.

Several years ago I was preaching in Arkansas and brought a series of messages on prayer during the noon-hour services. One day a distressed couple talked to me about their daughter who had left home in rebellion. They had no idea where she was or what she was doing, and imagined the very worst. They had become quite bitter because they had prayed as best as they knew how according to biblical guidelines, but to no avail. When I asked them what they were praying, they looked shocked that I would even have to ask.

"Why, we are praying that she will come home immediately, of course," they said. Then, they added, "And that is the primary prayer of our heart as you have been teaching us to pray."

I explained to them," I don't think that is truly your primary prayer. What you want more than anything in all the world is for your daughter to be safe and to be right with God and her loved ones. You feel, understandably, that if you can just get her home again, you will be able to secure her physical and spiritual welfare, so you are praying that she will come home immediately, period. But, the problem is that you don't know what's happening in her life right now. It's very possible that she may be on the verge of developing relationships with some people who can help her to straighten out her life permanently. If God answers your prayer to get her home immediately, he may have to tear her away from the very circumstances or persons he is using to accomplish your primary desire for your daughter. It's all right to pray for her to come home, but don't make it the primary prayer. Leave God free to work out his will and your heart's desire in whatever way necessary."

In a lighter vein, I remember a comic strip lesson from many years ago. It was during that time when Daisy Mae was endlessly pursuing Li'l Abner, with no indication that she would ever get him to the marriage altar. Mammy Yokum, Li'l Abner's mother, was getting terribly impatient with her reluctant son, and decided it was time for her to set him down and just tell him plainly it was time for him to marry Daisy Mae. So, Mammy went into one of her trances in which she was able to make direct contact with any Yokum she wanted to talk to. She sent out her powerful mental telepathy with the urgent message to Li'l Abner: "Drop whatever you are doing and come home to Mammy at once!"

What Mammy did not know was that her son had finally gotten up his nerve, on his own, and was at that very moment holding Daisy Mae in his arms, with the words of proposal on the tip of his tongue. When Mammy's message hit him, he did exactly what she commanded, literally dropped what he was doing (which happened to be Daisy Mae) and ran home to Mammy. Not only was Mammy unsuccessful in her pleading, but Li'l Abner lost his nerve completely and decided to go fishing instead of getting married.

If we wanted to make a religious illustration out of this episode, we would say that Mammy's primary prayer was for Li'l Abner to marry Daisy Mae, and her secondary prayer was for him to come home so she could tell him to do it. It would have been all right to suggest the secondary plan, but where she fouled up was in using her ESP powers to force her way, which wasn't the best way after all.

On the other hand, just as we can become obsessed with making the secondary prayer succeed, we can also become obsessed with forcing the fulfillment of the primary prayer. Abraham is known as the father of faith and deservedly so, but even the devoted Abraham and Sarah became impatient and decided to do God's work for him. God had promised Abraham, "I will make you exceeding fruitful, and I will make nations of you and kings shall come out of you" (Genesis 17:6). In her old age, Sarah was convinced that she would never bear children, and persuaded Abraham to fulfill his divine destiny by having a child by Sarah's maid Hagar. But, God had said, "Sarah thy wife shall bear thee a son indeed; and thou shalt call his name Isaac: and I will establish my covenant with him for an everlasting covenant, and with his seed after him" (Gen. 17:19). The resulting tension between Ishmael (Hagar's son) and Isaac (Sarah's son) continues even to this day in the tragic conflict between the Arabs and Jews. Abraham and Sarah were so determined that the primary promise be fulfilled that they stepped in to do God's work for him, contrary to his specific and revealed plans.

It is one thing to believe in God's plans and promises, and it is another thing to try stubbornly to force the execution of those plans and promises. God unquestionably wants people everywhere to come to him in faith: "The

Lord is . . . not willing that any should perish, but that all should come to repentance" (2 Peter 3:9). This could easily be called a primary purpose of God, and any Christian and any church is in line with biblical principles to make praying for the lost a primary prayer. There is, however, a grave danger in playing Abraham and Sarah's game when we are so eager to secure conversions that we will use any methods to manipulate and intimidate people, even small children, into making professions of faith. Whether working through a primary or secondary prayer, we must at all times keep from playing God.

5. SECONDARY PRAYERS ARE NOT MORE IMPORTANT THAN THEIR SCRIPTURAL MOTIVE

Specific biblical instructions are undoubtedly primary. For instance, the model prayer, called the Lord's Prayer, plainly outlines petitions we can comfortably pray because Christ himself told us to. In addition, he gave other directions for praying: "The harvest truly is plenteous, but the labourers are few; pray ye therefore the Lord of the harvest, that he will send forth labourers into his harvest" (Matt. 9:37, 38). Thus, we know a primary, biblically-based prayer would be for God to send the workers we need in the spiritual harvest.

It would be natural, also, for us to start praying for certain kinds of workers, or even for certain individuals, to be sent to us. We must keep in mind, though, that the important issue is the gathering of the harvest, not the person doing the work. Paul reminded us that one plants, another waters, but God gives the increase (1 Cor. 3:5-9).

A very spiritually minded friend once told us that she had prayed and prayed that a certain man would become her pastor, and she did not understand why that prayer was not answered. The reason she wanted him as pastor was because she honestly believed that he would do the best job possible for that church. Actually, then, her primary prayer was for the welfare of the church, and she wanted the best available pastor possible. She thought she knew who that person was, but she had to defer to the wisdom of Almighty God with his storehouse full of qualified preachers. Her real prayer, her primary prayer, was not unanswered. God was taking care of her church, but through a different leader than she had envisioned.

Preachers also can confuse their primary calling with a secondary field. It is certainly a biblical injunction to "make full proof of your ministry" (2 Tim. 4:5), so it would be a correct spiritual primary prayer for a preacher to pray that God would use him to his fullest capacity. The prayer begins to have human, secondary characteristics when he starts to tell God *where* he can do his best service.

I have come to believe that our primary calling is to *what* God wants us to be, and the *how* and *where* are secondary. Praying to know the how and where is necessary in our search to know God's will, but we should not despair of fulfilling his primary plan for our lives because the dream of a particular place or position has eluded us.

Mrs. Bill (Ruth) Pitts of Waco, Texas, is an outstanding example of one who has discovered that God's *what* for our lives must come before his *where*. Ruth was born with all four limbs severely impaired. She had a total of four fingers, two on each hand. Her right leg was missing and her left leg was bent and crooked. The first four years of her life were spent in hospitals where she was given an additional artificial finger on her right hand, and her left leg was straightened.

Ruth's parents, Dr. and Mrs. James Landes, have been strong leaders in pastoral, academic, and denominational ministries. Very early in life Ruth felt called to special service, with a particular yearning for foreign missions. During her freshman year in college she corresponded with a foreign mission board, and was greatly disappointed to learn that the board could not send people with physical handicaps to the foreign mission field.

Ruth became more involved in her music courses and eventually majored in music education. She became an accomplished pianist, soloist, and music teacher. She and her husband, Bill Pitts, both received their Ph.D. degrees and taught in several Baptist universities. Ruth continued, however, to be disappointed that she had not been able to go to the foreign mission field, and felt very dissatisfied with her contribution to the Lord's work.

In 1980, Ruth, Bill, and their two sons went to Recife, Brazil, for a short missions service. They taught in the seminary there and Ruth conducted associational music schools. In Brazil, Ruth had a dramatic awakening to the reality of God's call and working in her life. Her own words describe it beautifully: "I was somewhat surprised to find that the missionaries (and I was a temporary missionary) worked in the same manner in Brazil as I did every day in Waco, Texas, teaching piano and voice to young men and women, working with youth choirs, etc. I returned home much more satisfied with my work. I am now certain that the Lord called me to witness through music and that the place is of little importance."

6) SECONDARY PRAYERS SHOULDN'T BLOCK A BETTER SOLUTION

One of the great bonuses of the Christian life is to be surprised again and again that what God finally gives us is better than we originally asked for.

A few years ago I became critically ill with numerous neurological symptoms. I was diagnosed by many reputable doctors as having multiple sclerosis. I began to deteriorate rapidly, with the symptoms increasing in number and severity. Within a few months I could barely walk, even with a cane, and had to preach sitting down. It became obvious that I was not going to be able to continue a normal pastorate. I had been struck down in the prime of life and in the midst of a busy, thriving ministry. How to pray? Of course, many well-intentioned friends insisted that I should prove my faith and pray for healing. Indeed, many of them were praying for my healing to demonstrate the power of God.

During all that time of agony and uncertainty, I had one clear, conscious primary prayer, "Lord, please let me live long enough and well enough to finish what you put me here to do."

Of course, we had many secondary prayers during those long months, and some were granted and some were not. In answer to specific needs, God sent unexpected financial help several times, three different airplanes were placed at our disposal to fly to medical centers for treatment, emotional and spiritual encouragement were supplied on every hand, and fellow ministers took over many of the chores I could no longer perform. But, there were some secondary prayers which were not answered.

As I began to accept the inevitable decision of having to leave the pastorate, I began to pray for mechanical means to help me function: a wheelchair, an electric typewriter, a tape recorder or dictaphone, etc. We were not able to secure by any means a single one of these physical things I thought I had to have. The only reason I was praying for certain things was in order to fulfill my primary desire to complete the ministry God wanted me to do, and it seemed certain it could not be as a pastor.

As usual, God knew something none of us knew. Through several sudden occurrences we discovered that I did not have multiple sclerosis, but instead I have five herniated discs which were causing all the neurological symptoms and physical impairment. After three successful back surgeries, and several long months of recuperation, I was back in the role of active pastor and preacher.

Many of our friends, family, and church members were frustrated during my ordeal. They could not understand why God was refusing to hear the many prayers for my healing, and I was often discouraged when some of my own prayers for what I thought were genuine needs were not granted. Yet, I kept praying my basic, primary prayer, believing that in his own way and time God would give me the assurance that he had done with my life what he had intended. That may sound very vague, but at the time it was very real to me. I knew exactly what it was that I was feeling and praying, but I could never have guessed that God was going to answer in such a marvelous way. I shudder to think how impoverished I would be if I had been willing to settle for one of those secondary requests when God was able and willing to give me not only my primary

Secondary Prayer: How Do You Want It Done?

request, but a whole new lease on life to enjoy its fulfillment.

Think about the prayers which you now have "pending" before God. Which of these can you readily identify as secondary, and which truly qualify for primary status?

One of Charles Shultz's *Peanuts* characters, Linus, expressed his desire to be a humble, wealthy, highly successful country doctor. Then he added, "with a red sports car." It's pretty easy to spot the secondary request of Linus. It may not be as easy to identify your secondary prayers, but it is essential to understanding what is going on in your prayer relationship with God. What you may have been writing off as "unanswered" prayers may be secondary requests which do not implement a positive answer to your primary request, which is still "pending." You may conclude that your *real* prayer hasn't been unanswered after all, that God is still at work behind the scenes.

The symbol below is the start of developing a visual image of praying in harmony. Other symbols will be added as the image evolves. The square (strong, stable, sure) represents your primary prayer. The arrows shooting off in many directions represent your secondary prayers. They are all connected in some way to the primary prayer, but some are much closer to it than others. How close is your latest secondary prayer to the real desire of your heart and the center of your life?

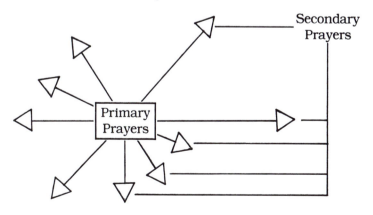

CHAPTER THREE
MOTIVE PRAYER:
Why Do You Want It?

"Your requests are not granted because you pray from wrong motives, to spend what you get on your pleasures" (James 4:3).

Certain kinds of praying enable us to put all our prayers in harmony with each other. First, there was primary prayer, which expresses *what* we desire foremost and earnestly. Then, there was secondary prayer, which expresses *how* we think our desire can best be consummated. Now, there is motive prayer, *why* we want the request in the first place. When we honestly examine our prayers with the tests of what, how, and why, we are able to see whether our prayers harmonize, and where we need to pray differently.

Motive undergirds all prayers. It is the basic foundation upon which all lives of faith are built. It is the fabric woven into every garment of righteousness. Motive is foremost of all primary prayers. After you have settled on *what* is the most important thing for you to ask of God, you still must answer *why* it is most important to you. The motive for your request reveals the character and quality of your religious faith and your personal relationship with God.

When Jesus said, "Whatsoever ye shall ask in my

name, that will I do, that the Father may be glorified in the Son" (John 14:13), he gave this promise within the context of a larger discussion. An important rule for interpreting Scripture is to study it in the light of the immediate context.

Although several famous quotations are lifted out of John 14, the essential topic of that discourse is that of *relationship*. Jesus began by saying, "Ye believe in God, believe also in me" (v. 1). After that, all references to God are made in terms of the family relationship. "In my Father's house are many mansions" (v. 2). "No man cometh unto the Father, but by me" (v. 6). "If ye had known me, ye should have known my Father also" (v. 7). "He that hath seen me hath seen the Father" (v. 9). "I am in the Father, and the Father in me . . . the Father who dwells in me does the works" (v. 10). "Believe me that I am in the Father, and the Father in me: or else believe me for the very works' sake" (v. 11). "He that believeth on me, the works that I do shall he do also; and greater works than these shall he do; because I go unto my Father" (v. 12). Then, comes the next verse of prayer promise: "Whatsoever you shall ask in my name, that I will do, that the Father may be glorified in the Son" (v. 13).

Relationship is the key word in this entire section, the relationship of the Son to the Father. Every promise, whether it relates to mansions in heaven, ability to perform mighty works, or power to get what we pray for, is directly connected to the Father-Son relationship of God and Jesus. Too many people have tried to claim the promise of verse 14 ("If you shall ask anything in my name, I will do it") without realizing that it is vitally and unalterably connected to the primary motive of verse 13: "that the Father may be glorified in the Son."

What does it mean to be "glorified"? In Hebrew the word glory is *kabod* and in Greek it is *doxa*. From the Greek word we get our musical designation of "doxology." When we sing our doxologies we are praying for, and paying homage to, the divine presence or glory of God. The glory of God means more than a glittering majesty. It means the very essence of God himself.

In both the Hebrew and the Greek, the word we translate "glory" means "presence, weight, or substance." It means more than the fact that one can answer the roll call that he is present. It means that his presence is obvious and materially experienced by all. In the tribal councils of Israel, a venerable father of faith would stride in with great *kabod*, and the people would know that a respected presence and a voice to be heard was among them. In the Greek empires a prominent landowner or a famous warrior would stand to speak in the assemblies, and all would feel his *doxa*, his weight, his substance, his presence.

When God is glorified, his presence is obvious. Men are consciously aware that there is a God dynamically at work in his world. When Jesus promised to give what we ask, he said it would be on the condition that the Father would be glorified, that the world would know that God is present.

How does that happen? The same way it happened during Jesus' life. In the setting of the verses we are studying in John 14, Philip said to Jesus, "Lord, shew us the Father, and it sufficeth us." Jesus answered, "Have I been so long time with you, Philip, and yet hast thou not known me? He that hath seen me hath seen the Father . . . I am in the Father, and the Father is in me . . . the Father that dwelleth in me, he doeth the works." God was glorified (his presence manifest and his work accomplished) in the person of Jesus. When men saw Jesus, they saw the Father. That is, they were aware of God's weight, substance, presence—his glory.

Jesus went on to say, "He that believeth in me, the works that I do shall he do also; and greater works than these shall he do" (John 14:12). How is that possible? The same way the great works of Jesus were possible. He said that it was the Father dwelling in him who actually did the works. If we do the works of Christ, it will also be because the Father is dwelling in us and working through us by the living presence of Christ. This is the spirit of

Paul's great declaration: "I am crucified with Christ: nevertheless I live; yet not I, but Christ liveth in me: and the life which I now live in the flesh I live by the faith of the Son of God" (Gal. 2:20).

What this verse reveals is the pattern of a life-style dedicated to God's glory. The motive prayer of the Christian is not simply adding the thought that this request is made "for the glory of God," or "for his sake" as we often say. It is perfectly all right and appropriate for us to use such words in our spoken prayers, but they should be the mere reflection of a larger life-style. "Whatsoever ye do, do all to the glory of God" (1 Cor. 10:31). The whole life, in all its parts, is given up to God's glory, and then we can really pray to his glory also.

Prayer is not one isolated activity or compartment of life; it is the representative expression of the total life. A motive prayer expresses the motive life. What motivates me in my daily living is the real motivation of my verbalized prayer. If I am living for self-glory, to make the world aware of my "weight, substance, and presence," that is also what I am wanting to accomplish with my prayer, regardless of how many times I repeat the formula, "for thy glory and thy sake."

Prayer should be the one area in which the question of whose glory we seek is settled. If we are praying, it is because we recognize that we are dependent on God. The prayer itself should serve as a testimony to God's glory. This is the sense and substance of Paul's query to the Corinthians: "What hast thou that thou didst not receive? Now if thou didst receive it, why dost thou glory, as if thou hadst not received it?" (1 Cor. 4:7). Yet, some people glory in their "prayer power." They are constantly telling how they have changed things and people by their prayers. They have made prayer to appear a work of man rather than receiving it as a gift of God.

The emphasis must be placed on the total life-style. To live for the glory of God means that deep down in your soul, your main reason for living is to demonstrate the presence of the Father at work in his world. When you achieve or excel, you rejoice that others will be made aware of the reality of God through your achievement. When you sin, your greatest fear is not of being caught or being punished, but of bringing reproach upon the name of Christ which the world associates with you. When you pray, you want only that request which will in some way bring honor and glory to the name of Christ, will make the power of God more readily seen by men, and will uphold the principles of God's Word.

When this wholeness of purpose exists God is being glorified in us even before we consciously ask it. When Jesus was praying about his approaching death on the cross, he said he would not ask God to save him from this hour. Instead, he prayed, "Father glorify thy name." Then a voice came from heaven, saying, "I have both glorified it, and will glorify it again" (John 12:27, 28).

God is glorified in the life that is living for him, even before a prayer request is made. Wouldn't it be simple logic to suppose that the prayer from such a life would be the kind of prayer most likely to be granted?

In the middle of the nineteenth century a German-born Britisher by the name of George Müller astonished the world with his simplistic commitment to the prayer promises of Christ. Believing that temporal as well as spiritual needs could be supplied through faith and prayer, he abolished pew rents and refused a salary, supporting himself and his charitable work with offerings from his followers. Then he moved to Bristol where he devoted his life to the care of orphan children, relying completely on voluntary contributions. Starting with only a few children, he eventually had 2,000 under his care. The work was continued year after year in a simple fashion. When there was a need, George Müller took the need to God in prayer, and forthrightly that need was met. Striking stories of uncanny "coincidences" came regularly from the Bristol orphanage. Through the years it has been supposed that Müller was simply a great man of faith. There was something else also, which has to come even before faith. George Müller explains it very clearly in his own words:

I had constantly cases brought before me, which proved that one of the especial things which the children of God needed in our day, was to have their faith strengthened.

I longed, therefore, to have something to point my brethren to, as a visible proof that our God and Father is the same faithful God as ever He was; as willing as ever to prove Himself to be the living God in our day as formerly, to all who put their trust in Him.

My spirit longed to be instrumental in strengthening their faith, by giving them not only instances from the word of God, of His willingness and ability to help all who rely upon Him, but to show them by proofs that He is the same in our day. I knew that the word of God ought to be enough, and it was by grace enough for me; but still I considered I ought to lend a helping hand to my brethren.

I therefore judged myself bound to be the servant of the Church of Christ, in the particular point in which I had obtained mercy; namely, in being able to take God at His word and rely upon it. The first object of the work was, and is still: that God might be magnified by the fact that the orphans under my care are provided with all they need, only by prayer and faith, without any one being asked; thereby it may be seen that God is faithful still, and hears prayer still.

I have again these last days prayed much about the Orphan House, and have frequently examined my heart; that if it were at all my desire to establish it for the sake of gratifying myself, I might find it out. For as I desire only the Lord's glory, I shall be glad to be instructed by the instrumentality of my brother, if the matter be not of Him.

When I began the Orphan work in 1835, my chief object was the glory of God, by giving a practical demonstration as to what could be accomplished simply through the instrumentality of prayer and faith, in order thus to benefit the Church at large, and to lead a careless world to see the reality of the things of God, by showing them in this work, that the living God is still, as 4000 years ago, the living God. This my aim has been abundantly honoured. Multitudes of sinners have been thus converted, multitudes of the children of God in all parts of the world have been benefited by this work, even as I had anticipated. But the larger the work has grown, the greater has been the blessing, bestowed in the very way in which I looked for blessing: for the attention of hundreds of thousands has been drawn to the work; and many tens of thousands have come to see it. All this leads me to desire further and further to labour on in this way, in order to bring yet greater glory to the name of the Lord. That He may be looked at, magnified, admired, trusted in, relied on at all times, is my aim in this service; and so particularly in this intended enlargement. That it may be seen how much one poor man, simply by trusting in God, can bring about by prayer; and that thus other children of God may be led to carry on the work of God in dependence upon Him; and that children of God may be led increasingly to trust in Him in their individual positions and circumstances, therefore I am led to this further enlargement.

George Müller's life-style of prayer is a superb example of all three elements of prayers in harmony with each other. The primary prayer of caring for those orphaned children was most definitely in line with biblical guidelines, and represented the total commitment of Müller's life. The secondary prayers were consistent with the aims of the primary prayer, and still left the method and means in the prerogative of God. The motive prayer undergirding every effort and every request was for God to be glorified.

I was as impressed with what Müller did *not* say as what he did say about his motivation. If most of us were to be asked about the motivation for such a venture, we would probably say that the motivation was obviously to care for homeless children. That is a high and worthy cause, but notice as you read back through Müller's statement that he did not say that he was started on his great life's work because of his love for little children or his compassion for the oppressed. The deep motivating force of his life was to see God honored and believed in. Supplying the orphans' needs was not an end unto itself; it was the means by which he was able to call the world's attention to the power and the love of God.

The motive of your prayer is known only to you and God. Even though you may tell someone what your motive is, the telling can never quite equal the feeling. It may be difficult to put it into words, but you can know in your own heart why you really want what you have prayed for. You may need to pray for wisdom where your motive is concerned. Before you start praying for specific things, you might profit immeasurably by asking God to reveal your own heart to your conscious mind. Of course, you will have to be both honest and brave to do this. If you are not able and willing to face the truth about your real and raw motives, that may be the reason you have not been satisfied in your prayer life. God can best reveal himself to those who are willing to have themselves revealed. We must be willing to admit that the thought of our joy or our pleasure was far stronger than any yearnings for God's glory. Some of us may never have thought of God's glory at all.

Life abhors a vacuum, and rushes in to fill that vacuum with something, usually the most accessible substance. If God does not get the glory, someone else will, and therein lies one of the most serious consequences. Human beings begin to give and receive glory among themselves, putting God aside and robbing themselves of his presence and power. The rushing in of human glory to fill the vacuum where God's glory is absent makes faith an impossibility. Jesus asked, "How can ye believe, which receive honour one of another, and seek not the honour that cometh from God only?" (John 5:44).

Although he was the Son of God and affirmed that he and the Father were one, Jesus humbly said, "I seek not mine own glory" (John 8:50). He would not allow any glory, not even his own, to replace the Father's glory. He came to the end of his life saying, "I have glorified thee on earth: I have finished the work which thou gavest me to do" (John 17:4). If Jesus Christ existed and prayed only for the glory of God, how much more should we sinners live only for his glory: "If any man speak, let him speak as the oracles of God; if any man minister, let him do it as of the ability which God giveth; that God in all things may be glorified through Jesus Christ" (1 Peter 4:11).

Now we add another part to our symbol, which represents prayers in harmony. The large circle around both secondary and primary prayers is the motive behind all prayers.

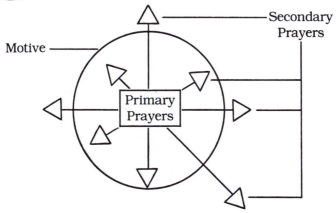

Ideally, all prayers, whether primary or secondary, should be within the circle of the right motive, which is to glorify God. Realistically, however, some of the secondary prayers are closer to the primary prayer than others, and some of them are inside the right motive (glorifying God), some of them are outside, and some are sort of borderline.

It should be noted also that all primary prayers are not directly in the center of the right motive. We mentioned earlier that the primary, consuming passion of life may lie outside biblical principles and the will of God. So, a diagram of some of your prayers which are not in perfect harmony might look more like this:

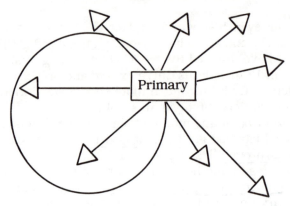

In this diagram we see a primary prayer which is just barely within the motive of glorifying God, and several secondary prayers going in random directions. The ironical thing is that some secondary prayers are more within the right motive than the primary prayer which was behind them.

Ideally, however, what you should strive for is a picture of harmony. You want to pray in such a way that you will have the right motive and make specific requests which will be in harmony with your primary prayer based on God's Word and will.

Visualize a symbol of harmony, which depicts all the elements of prayer working together.

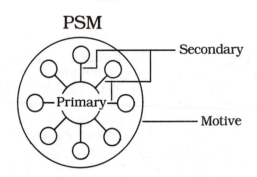

In this symbol the larger, perfect circle remains the motive prayer (M) to glorify God. At the center is the primary prayer (P) which has also become a circle. Sometimes the hard corners of our basic determination need to be smoothed and rounded off to comply with the larger motive. Even the primary prayer must submit to and conform to the contours of the motive prayer. Then the smaller circles are the secondary prayers (S) which are no longer sharp arrows darting where they please. They are now uniform extensions of the primary prayer, and they have also assumed the circular shape of the motive prayer. Thus, a perfect circle in balanced harmony, with the letters PSM (Primary, Secondary, Motive) above becomes our completed symbol for prayers that are in harmony with each other.

Now that we have examined the inner and related harmony of the prayers themselves, we need to see what other elements in our praying need the touch of harmony.

PART

2

Pray in Harmony with God

"And when Love speaks, the voice of all the gods Make heaven drowsy with the harmony."

WILLIAM SHAKESPEARE
Love's Labor Lost

PRAYER is a gift from God. In his infinite wisdom and sovereign grace, the Creator of all things has given man the privilege of communicating with him. Since prayer originates with God, and not with man, it is only right that we should pray in harmony with the One who has made it possible for us to pray.

You must always keep God at the heart and center of your prayers. The primary focus cannot be on your need or desire, but on him who alone can meet that need and grant that desire. When the thing you are praying for takes center stage over God, you are out of harmony with the Giver of all things.

Even the prayer itself cannot be the focal point of your faith. Although we are told repeatedly in the Scriptures to pray, even to "pray without ceasing," our faith is not to be anchored in the activity or exercise of praying. Jesus' powerful teaching on the importance of faith in praying is introduced by his emphatic command, "Have faith in God" (Mark 11:22-24).

Our faith is not to be in our own ability or worthiness, nor in the fact that we have obediently prayed as commanded. God, and God alone, is to be the object of our faith. We believe not because of who we are, but because of who he is. We believe not because we have asked, but because he has the power to give. We believe not in man's work in prayer, but in God's grace in answering.

These two aspects of prayer—that prayer is a gift from God, and that our faith is to be in God alone—make it essential that our prayers be in harmony with God, even as God is in harmony with himself.

God is one! "Hear, O Israel, the Lord our God is one Lord" (Deut. 6:4). Jesus repeated this as "the first of all the commandments" in Mark 12:29. Paul spoke of "one Lord, one God and Father of all" (Eph. 4:5, 6; See also 1 Cor. 8:4, 1 Tim. 2:5).

When the Christian speaks of the Trinity he does not mean three gods, he means a triune (three in one) God. There is only one God, and he has chosen to reveal himself in three ways, as Father, Son, and Holy Spirit. "For there are three that bear record in heaven, the Father, the Word, and the Holy Ghost: and these three are one" (1 John 5:7).

Therefore, if you are going to pray to the Christian God who has revealed himself to mankind, you need to know enough about each of these three revelations to pray in harmony with the fullness of God. Each revelation has a specific and vital part in the communication between God and man.

CHAPTER FOUR
IN HIS POWER:
The Heavenly Father

"Then the omnipotent Father with
his thunder made Olympus tremble."

OVID, *Metamorphoses*

"Our God is in the heavens: he hath
done whatsoever he hath pleased" (Psalm 115:3).

Behind every request we ever make is the assumption or the hope that the person we are asking has the ability to grant our request. It would be a waste of time and intelligence to keep expecting something from someone we know to be incapable of giving it.

Children naturally turn to their parents in time of need, confident that they can meet the need. Jesus was making effective use of this natural tendency when he told us to pray, "Our Father, which art in heaven."

When God reveals himself as heavenly Father he causes us to think of many fatherly attributes and activities: creation, provision, control, wisdom, benevolence, judgment, punishment, forgiveness, ownership, and relationship.

All of these could probably be best summed up in the word *power.* The child sees in all the father's activities a power beyond his own, and he senses that the father has freedom to use that power.

The heavenly Father to whom we pray is a God of power and might (1 Chron. 29:12). The psalmist said that all power belongs unto God (Ps. 62:11). Jesus underscored the power of God by saying that "with God all things are possible" (Matt. 19:26). When Gabriel told Mary that although she was a virgin she would be the mother of Christ, he concluded, "For with God nothing shall be impossible" (Luke 1:37).

Before you rush to your prayer closet and start demanding "impossible" things from God, remember that all prayer must be in harmony with the character and purpose of God himself. Power does not merely mean brute force that can make things happen. As you contemplate the marvelous power of God, consider carefully what real power is.

POWER IS THE ABILITY TO ACHIEVE PURPOSE

Before you word the prayer that calls upon the heavenly Father to put all the power of the universe (which is his) at your disposal, remember that he is not simply a cosmic force to be activated by turning the right key. He is a God of wisdom as well as a God of power. "Blessed be the name of God for ever and ever: for wisdom and might are his" (Dan. 2:20).

Our magnificent universe was not created by cosmic chance or by mindless power. It was produced through an infinite intelligence with a perfect purpose. "The Lord by wisdom hath founded the earth; by understanding hath he established the heavens" (Prov. 3:19). "O Lord, how manifold are thy works! In wisdom hast thou made them all" (Ps. 104:24).

Within the creative wisdom of God there is an eternal purpose, and behind that purpose is the unlimited power of God to accomplish his purpose.

God will accomplish his purpose for his world. Although the divine purpose may appear frustrated and stalled at times, he will ultimately do as he has purposed. "For the Lord of hosts hath purposed, and who shall disannul it?"

(Isa. 14:27). "For every purpose of the Lord shall be performed" (Jer. 51:29).

> *This is my Father's world,*
> *O let me ne'er forget*
> *That though the wrong seems oft so strong,*
> *God is the Ruler yet.*
> *This is my Father's world,*
> *The battle is not done;*
> *Jesus who died shall be satisfied,*
> *And earth and heav'n be one.*

This familiar hymn by Maltbie Babcock expresses poetically the divine purpose of God as given in Ephesians 1:9-12: "For God has allowed us to know the secret of his plan, and it is this: he purposed long ago in his sovereign will that all human history should be consummated in Christ, that everything that exists in heaven or earth should find its perfection and fulfillment in him. In Christ we have been given an inheritance, since we were destined for this, by the One who works out all his purposes according to the design of his own will. So that we, in due time, as the first to put our hope in Christ, may bring praise to his glory!" (Phillips).

As you approach God in prayer, reflect on the thoughts from the several Scriptures we have quoted:

1. The God to whom we pray is our heavenly Father.
2. As Father, he has all power and might, and nothing is impossible for him.
3. He is also a Father of wisdom and purpose.
4. The Father has the intention and power to accomplish his purposes.
5. The ultimate purpose of the Father is to unite all creation in the perfection of Christ.
6. Our part in his purpose is to bring praise to his glory.

Does your prayer harmonize with the purpose of God even as it calls upon his power? Remember that the power of God must be in harmony with the purpose of God!

Since Jesus is the human revelation of God, it might

help you to relate to the purpose of God on human terms by studying this Scripture which explains the purpose for Christ coming into the world: "For this purpose the Son of God was manifested, that he might destroy the works of the devil" (1 John 3:8).

Does your prayer harmonize with this stated purpose of Christ? Remember, power is the ability to accomplish purpose. Is your request for God to use his power in your behalf in keeping with this stated purpose of Christ to destroy the works of Satan?

You may be thinking, if this is so, why is God so slow in conquering evil? Why doesn't he answer the many prayers to abolish war, crime, and suffering? Why did he permit Hitler to kill six million Jews? Why was slavery allowed to exist in America for 244 years? Why do unjustices go unchecked today?

These are legitimate questions that have a right to be asked in a book about prayer, and their answers may be found in some other straight questions: How does God accomplish his purpose? Does he work through force or persuasion? Is man a puppet or a free moral agent? Is it God's responsibility or man's to stop war and crime? Which is more permanent, to get man out of slavery or to get slavery out of men? (Do these questions remind you of our earlier point that primary prayer includes involvement?) We must not ask God to do what he has created us to do.

Imagine yourself as the coach for a team of small boys learning to play football. After watching your little fellows take a merciless beating from a larger team, you decide that they have had enough. You know they need your strength and experience. So, you stride on to the field, pick up the ball yourself, knock the opponents right and left, and carry the ball over for a touchdown. Now, that is power, and you have used it in behalf of those who really need it.

"But," you immediately object, "that is not right. That's not the purpose of the game. The coach is supposed to train and develop the team to do it themselves." Yes, and this is what we mean when we say that real power is not brute force. It is the ability to achieve purpose, and action which defeats purpose is weakness, not power. Praying for the Father to use his power for us must be in accordance with his purpose.

POWER IS THE AUTHORITY TO COMMAND

Fathers not only have the ability to do things, they also have the authority to command their children to do things. As we call upon our heavenly Father to exercise his power for us, we need to remember that his power also involves his authority over us.

You are probably familiar with the Great Commission, which Christ gave to the church recorded in Matthew 28:19, 20. You are also aware that he prefaced the commission with verse 18, "All power is given unto me in heaven and in earth."

The word used here for "power" is more accurately translated "authority," because it is that special kind of power. This is also followed not by a demonstration of powerful acts, but by a command to be obeyed. Jesus gave the commission because he had the authority (power) to do so.

If you want God's power to be available to you, you must be available to God's authority. You cannot expect God to command his creation to serve you if you have not obeyed his command to serve him.

One of the most important passages in the Bible on the matter of answered prayer is: "And whatsoever we ask, we receive of him, because we keep his commandments, and do those things that are pleasing in his sight" (1 John 3:22).

Although many prayer promises are not this explicit about the relationship between obedience and power in prayer, most of them convey the same implicit message. For instance, the well-known promise of James 5:16 says that "the effectual fervent prayer of a righteous man availeth much." What is a righteous man other than one who lives obediently in the righteousness of Christ?

Another prayer promise from Christ himself stated: "Ye

have not chosen me, but I have chosen you, and ordained you, and appointed you, that you should go and bring forth fruit, and that your fruit should remain: that whatsoever ye shall ask the Father in my name, he will give it you" (John 15:16).

It is clear that Jesus was linking obedient consecration to our calling (bearing fruit that lasts) to the promise of unlimited blessings.

Notice the concentration of the verses in John 14 which relate obedience to blessing. "If ye love me, keep my commandments. . . . and . . . the Father . . . shall give you another Comforter" (vv. 15, 16). "He that hath my commandments, and keepeth them, he it is that loveth me: and he that loveth me shall be loved of my Father, and I will love him, and manifest myself to him" (v. 21). "If a man loves me, he will keep my words: and my Father will love him, and we will come to him and make our abode with him" (v. 23).

Another principle of harmony in the ever-widening influence of prayer is your professed love for Christ, which must be in harmony with your response to his words. Your expectations of answered prayer must also be in harmony with your degree of obedient service.

Our answered prayers must also be followed by obedience. In other words, we can't obey God to get a prayer answered, and then quit obeying. After all, God not only knows what we have done but also what we will do.

Thus, the prayer and its expected answer should be in harmony with related principles which we will keep following. If we pray for money, we must intend to obey the Bible's precepts about responsibility and stewardship. If we pray for health, our continuing obedience will involve treating our bodies as the temple of God. If we pray for friends, our response to a positive answer must be one of love, service, and loyalty to them. If we pray for a church home, we must seek our place of service within the church God gives us. If we pray for divine guidance or spiritual wisdom, we must act accordingly when the way is made clear. Quite simply, if we ask God to reveal his will, then we must be willing to do his will when it is known.

The Father is not only to be respected for his power and sought for his purpose. He is also to be obeyed for his authority. It is in the doing of God's will that we discover the knowledge of God's power (John 7:17).

3) POWER IS THE CONSISTENCY OF CHARACTER

Another expression of genuine power is the ability to remain steadfast and sure when everything else is changing. In *The Lovely Ambition*, Mary Ellen Chase wrote, "My father was not interested in trying to prove God's existence. He simply staked all that he had, and was, on a tremendous gamble that God lived and moved among us and that his active concern for his world and for all his creatures was constant, invulnerable, and unfailing."

As you think about how to pray in harmony with God's power, think of God as the Father who remains constant and unfailing for his children. The most stable and mature adults are generally those who, as children, had the security of dependable and predictable parents. The most stable Christians are also those who have grown up with the concept of an unchanging God.

When the children know the nature, personality, ability, and limitations of their father, they know what kind of requests to make of him. If he remains consistent in those respects, they can have consistent expectations without undue disappointment.

One summer, when our children were rather young, we took a small boy into our home for several months. The first time we all went to a nice restaurant together, the boy waited for me to order for him. I told him that he could order for himself, just as our children did, and to get whatever he wanted. Our own children had been with us many times to eat in restaurants, they knew the limits of daddy's pocketbook, and they ordered accordingly. The new boy knew nothing about our eating habits or financial resources, and took me literally at my word. I had told him he could order anything he wanted, and he did just that, the biggest and most expensive steak on the menu. He was terribly embarrassed when I told him that it was more than I could afford. I had mishandled the situation and felt bad about causing his embarrassment.

Our heavenly Father is more considerate than I was. He has openly and constantly revealed himself to his children. Anyone who really wants to can pray in harmony with the nature and character of God, for his Word, his world, and his actions faithfully represent him. However, someone may hear only that Jesus has said, "Ask whatsoever you will," and take that to mean literally to order anything on the menu without any thought of the Father's nature. There are many things in this world (on the menu) that I will not ask the Father to give me because I know it would be inconsistent with his character and his way of doing things.

Praying in harmony with the Father's power of consistent character involves (1) determining his consistency, and (2) learning his character. Nature and history will offer you abundant testimony for both points, but since all prayer must harmonize with the biblical revelation, you need to know the Bible's testimony.

The psalmist testified of God, "Thou art the same, and thy years shall have no end" (Ps. 102:27). In Malachi, God said of himself, "I am the Lord, I change not" (Mal. 3:6).

The writer of Hebrews described the end of the world and the dissolving of the heavens: "And as a vesture shalt thou fold them up, and they shall be changed; but thou art the same, and thy years shall not fail" (Heb. 1:12). The same writer also referred to "Jesus Christ the same yesterday, and today, and forever" (Heb. 13:8). James specifically related the gifts of life (as in answered prayer) to the immutability (unchangeableness) of God: "Every good gift and every perfect gift is from above, and cometh down from the Father of lights, with whom is no variableness, neither shadow of turning" (James 1:17).

One of the most reassuring passages in the Bible is: "The eternal God is thy refuge, and underneath are the everlasting arms" (Deut. 33:27).

The Bible abounds with such references as these to the consistency and constancy of the heavenly Father. If he does not change, then we need to know what he is like so we can pray in harmony with his character.

God is holy, so we must never pray for anything that would compromise his holiness or cause us to be unholy (Ps. 99:9; Isa. 6:3; Rev. 15:4; Lev. 11:45; 1 Peter 1:16).

God is love, and our prayers should both invoke the love of God for others and reflect the love of God in our own attitudes (Jer. 31:3; John 3:16; Rom. 5:8; Eph. 2:4; 1 John 3:1).

God is good, and the results of our prayers must bring goodness into the lives of all concerned (Ps. 25:8; Ps. 33:5; Ps. 34:8; Nahum 1:7; Matt. 19:17; Rom. 2:4).

God is merciful, and our prayers should reflect that we have received his mercy and are willing to be merciful ourselves (Ps. 108:4; Lam. 3:22; Joel 2:13; Micah 7:18; Titus 3:5).

God is jealous, and we dare not ask for something that would take first place in our hearts over God (Exod. 20:5; Deut. 4:24; Josh. 24:19; 1 Kings 14:22; 1 Cor. 10:22).

God is just, and we cannot expect him to grant a request that would be unjust or unfair to anyone (Ps. 103:6; Zeph. 3:5; John 5:30; Rom. 2:2; Prov. 21:3; Rom. 13:7; Col. 4:1).

God is long-suffering, and neither our prayers nor our waiting for answers should show impatience toward him who is so patient with us (Isa. 48:9; Rom. 9:22; 1 Peter 3:20; 2 Peter 3:9; Col. 1:11).

God is truth, and our prayers must never seek to change or disguise truth (Deut. 32:4; 2 Sam. 7:28; Ps. 146:6; Rom. 3:4; Heb. 6:18).

God is peace, and we cannot ask him to grant that which would provoke strife and destroy righteous peace (Rom. 15:33; 2 Cor. 13:11; Phil. 4:9; 1 Thess. 5:23; Heb. 13:20; Col. 3:15).

God is impartial, and we should not ask selfishly for something we are not willing for the rest of God's children to have (Matt. 5:45; Acts 10:34, 35; Rom. 10:12; Gal. 2:6; Eph. 6:9).

Your prayers express not only your desires, but your

knowledge of and relationship to the Father. So, the more you know about the Father, and the closer your requests are to the consistent character of the Father, the greater can be your expectancy of getting what you pray for.

Your heavenly Father has all the power necessary to grant your prayer. But, remember that power involves purpose, authority, and constancy. Are you praying in harmony with these facets of God's power?

CHAPTER FIVE
IN HIS NAME:
The Human Son

"It is with literature as with
law or empire—an established
name is an estate in tenure or
a throne in possession."

EDGAR ALLAN POE, *Preface to Poems, 1831*

Our "problem" with having a heavenly Father is that he is heavenly! "God is spirit" and we physical earthlings cannot see him as we see ordinary objects in this world. We have the evidence of nature which we accept as his work. We have the testimony of prophets who claim to have heard his voice. We have the record of Scripture which proclaims his actions and purpose. But, we cannot see and hear *him!* The Bible admits this truth, but submits the invisibility of God as merely one of his attributes (Exod. 33;20; John 5:37; Col. 1:15; 1 Tim. 1:17; 6:16).

The Christian faith contends that God took human form two thousand years ago in the person of Jesus of Nazareth. The heart of the Christian gospel declares that "the Word was made flesh, and dwelt among us, (and we beheld his glory, the glory as of the only begotten of the Father,) full of grace and truth" (John 1:14).

John explained that the purpose for the incarnation (coming in the flesh) was to make the invisible God known to man: "No man hath seen God at any time; the only begotten Son, which is in the bosom of the Father, he hath declared him" (John 1:18).

Jesus himself plainly stated, "If ye had known me, ye should have known my Father also: and from henceforth ye know him, and have seen him. . . . He that hath seen me hath seen the Father" (John 14:7, 9).

It is very significant that these words of Jesus about his identity with the Father immediately precede his prayer promise, "Whatsoever ye shall ask in my name, that will I do, that the Father may be glorified in the Son. If ye shall ask anything in my name, I will do it" (John 14:13, 14).

This same prayer formula and promise is repeated in the next chapter: ". . . that your fruit should remain: that whatsoever ye shall ask of the Father in my name, he may give it you" (John 15:16). It comes up again in the next chapter: "I say unto you, whatsoever ye shall ask the Father in my name, he will give it you" (John 16:23). And again: "Hitherto have ye asked nothing in my name: ask, and ye shall receive, that your joy may be full" (John 16:24). And again: "At that day ye shall ask in my name" (John 16:26).

All of this adds up to a very important item in your prayer life. Many times Christians overlook the relationship between the incarnation and prayer. We know that Jesus came to redeem us, that "God was in Christ, reconciling the world unto himself" (2 Cor. 5:19). We know that the incarnation was God's means for our salvation through the humility, obedience, humiliation, death, and resurrection of Jesus (Phil. 2:5-11). The fact that he became a man assists us in praying. In fact, our prayer is not in complete harmony with God until we pray in the name of the human Son just as we pray in the power of the heavenly Father.

The big question before us is: What does it mean to pray "in his name?" Many Christians think they have fulfilled that requirement for answered prayer when they say at the end of some request, "This I ask in the name of Jesus Christ." There is certainly nothing wrong with repeating that familiar phrase, and most of us do it regularly. The mistake comes when we let the verbal phrase replace the real meaning behind it. A proper understanding of this phrase might help us to pray in harmony with God.

HIS NAME IS HIS NATURE

In the ancient world, a name did not merely distinguish a person from other persons, but was closely related to the nature of its bearer. This was particularly true in the case of deities. The name of a god was regarded as part of the being of the divinity which was so named because of his character and powers.

The Hebrews shared this ancient concept that the name possessed a much greater degree of reality and substance than as a mere sign of identification. In the Old Testament the sanctuary was spoken of as a place where God had chosen to cause his name to dwell (Exod. 20:24; Deut. 12:11). In this case the name was to be regarded as deity. In many cases the name of Jehovah simply indicated himself, as in, "Let them also that love thy name be joyful in thee" (Ps. 5:11; 7:17; 9:2, 18:49).

In the New Testament, the same application is used. It is God himself who is intended in such phrases as "Hallowed be thy name" (Matt. 6:9); "blaspheme his name" (Rev. 13:6); "in his name shall the Gentiles trust" (Matt. 12:21); "call on the name" (Acts 2:21); and "sing unto the name" (Rom. 15:9).

When Jesus said, "I manifested thy name unto the men whom thou gavest me" (John 17:6), the name implied God's nature and will. Paul was said to be "a chosen vessel to bear my name" (Acts 9:15), which means to represent God's mind and purpose.

Thus, to pray in Jesus' name means to pray in his nature, to pray in the character, spirit, and attitude of Jesus. You may begin, punctuate, and close every prayer with the phrase "in Christ's name," but it is not a bona fide Christian prayer unless it is in harmony with the nature of Jesus Christ.

Jesus was very plain and direct in teaching that the verbal use of his name was totally ineffective unless accompanied by the doing of his will. "Not every one that saith unto me, Lord, Lord, shall enter into the kingdom of heaven; but he that doeth the will of my Father which is in heaven. Many will say to me in that day, Lord, Lord, have we not prophesied in thy name? and in thy name cast out devils? and in thy name done many wonderful works? And then I will profess unto them, I never knew you: depart from me, ye that work iniquity" (Matt. 7:21-23).

How can you translate all of this into modern usage so you will know how to pray? Quite simply, is your prayer one that Jesus would pray in your circumstances? Considering his nature, attitude, and spirit, are you asking for the kind of things that Jesus Christ would ask for?

How can you know what Jesus would ask for? Again, we return to the Bible, our only source of information about Jesus. To know what Jesus would pray for, you need to know the very nature of Jesus as revealed in Scripture. "If ye abide in me, and my words abide in you, ye shall ask what ye will." Note the word "abide." You have to live with Christ to know him.

You also need to study the prayers which Christ himself prayed. There are seventeen references to Christ's personal prayer life and these could be grouped under four headings:

1. His prayers at the great events of his life: His baptism (Luke 3:21); the choice of the twelve (Luke 6:12); the confession of his messiahship (Luke 9:18); the transfiguration (Luke 9:29); in Gethsemane (Luke 22:39-46); and on the cross (Luke 23:46).

2. His prayers in the course of his ministry: before conflict with authorities (Luke 5:16); before giving the Model Prayer (Luke 11:1); when the Greeks came to him (John 12:27); and after feeding the five thousand (Mark 6:46).

3. His prayers at his miracles: healing the multitudes (Mark 1:35); feeding the five thousand (Mark 6:41); healing a deaf-mute (Mark 7:34); and raising Lazarus (John 11:41).

4. His prayers for others: for the eleven (John 17:6-19); for the whole church (John 17:20-26); for those who cru-

cified him (Luke 23:34); and for Peter (Luke 22:32).

Study the life and prayers of Jesus. Learn the spirit of Jesus. Pray in his nature, and you will be praying in his name. The heavenly Father is invisible, but the human Son became visible and left a historical record of what he is like. He also said that what he is like is what God is like. So, if you truly want to pray in harmony with God pray like Jesus would pray, approach the Father in the Son's name or nature.

HIS NAME IS HIS PRESENCE

While the name of God in the Bible referred generally to his nature or being, there were times when it indicated a specific presence. God told Israel that he was going to send an angel (special messenger) to lead them to the promised land. He instructed them to "beware of him, and obey his voice, provoke him not . . . for my name is in him" (Exod. 23:21).

Jesus said, "Where two or three are gathered together in my name, there am I in the midst of them" (Matt. 18:20). There you have it explicitly said, his name and his presence are synonymous. And, the significant fact is that that verse comes immediately after the prayer promise of verse 19 which says "that if two of you shall agree on earth as touching any thing that they shall ask, it shall be done for them of my Father which is in heaven."

These two verses must be taken together. Note the recurring theme of harmony. You pray in harmony with another Christian, "if two of you agree." You pray in harmony with Christ's nature, "together in my name." You pray in harmony with his presence, "there am I in the midst of them."

There is also another very exciting possibility for seeing his name as his presence. Paul wrote, "It is Christ that died, yea rather that is also risen, who is even at the right hand of God, who also maketh intercession for us" (Rom. 8:34; see also Heb. 7:25).

The presence of Christ is not only with and in his disciples as they pray in his name. The presence of Christ is also with the Father where he intercedes for us. It is as though he inspires the prayers in us, expresses them for us, accompanies them to the Father, and presents them in our behalf. He never leaves from the beginning to the consummation of the prayer process.

Once I ordered some goods which were important and had to be received quickly. I was told that it would have to be a "walk through" order. The salesman explained that he would personally carry my order to the manufacturer, walk through the construction process with them as they made it, and then personally hand deliver to me. Could this be something of the way Christ operates in our prayer life?

I have often heard illustrations which never quite satisfied me about praying in Christ's name. I have heard it compared to presenting a blank check to the Father with Christ's name signed. I have also heard it compared to the power of attorney which a businessman gives his employee to use in his behalf in his absence.

Now, I know why both of these illustrations fall short. They both assume the absence of Christ. One assumes his absence before the Father and I present a check in his name. The other assumes his absence on earth and I carry on in his name, or behalf. Both are so wrong! Christ is not absent in either earth or heaven. He is with us while we pray, and he is with the Father as he hears and answers our prayer. I do not know how it happens, but it must happen for our prayers to be in harmony both on earth and in heaven.

HIS NAME IS HIS RELATION

A name is one of the simplest ways to indicate relationship. Members of the same family carry the same name, signifying a mutual belonging and responsibility. Names are inherited from birth, with the child usually bearing the name of the natural father. Names are transferred through adoption, with the child assuming the name of the adopted parents. Names are changed by marriage, with the wife usually assuming the husband's family name.

In all of this, we are testifying to the world of a oneness, a union, a harmony. Ideally, each of these name unions, whether by birth, adoption, or marriage, speaks of a union of love and mutual trust. Common interests and common goals characterize those in a name union. Sharing of the family possessions also goes with the sharing of a name.

Suppose a bride whose life has been one of poverty marries a wealthy bridegroom. She gives up her own name, to be called by his, and now has the full right to use it. She purchases and acts in his name, which is honored by all. He trusts her to respect and use his name with integrity and honor. She trusts him to back her with all the resources of his good name. It is not because he is absent, but because they are now one.

The Bible uses the beautiful language of family and home to describe the believer's relationship to Christ. Those who believe on his name become the children of God (John 1:12). Jesus said that whoever does the will of the Father is his brother, sister, and mother (Luke 8:21). Sometimes this new relationship is spoken of as adoption by the Father (Rom. 8:15; Gal. 4:5). We are in the household of God (Eph. 2:19). We are a part of his whole family (Eph. 3:15). As his children, we are heirs of God and joint heirs with Christ (Rom. 8:17).

As members of his church, we are also referred to as the bride of Christ (Matt. 9:15; 25:6; John 3:29; 2 Cor. 11:2; Rev. 19:7; 21:2; 22:17). Whether using the analogy of children or as bride, the same significance of the union with his name is applicable.

When I bear another name (such as Christ's) it indicates that I have given up my own independent life. But, it also indicates that I have received in return all of his life and love and power. The name and the power of asking go together. When the name of Jesus completely possesses me and becomes the power that rules my life, then the power of his name in prayer will be mine also.

We are told to "*Ask* all" in Christ's name, but we are also told to "*Do* all in the name of the Lord Jesus" (Col. 3:17). To do all and to ask all in his name must go together. In a family, the child resembles and acts like his parents. In marriage, a husband and wife support each other and walk in harmony. Such must be our relation to the name of our Lord. If we do not reflect a family resemblance, if we do not bear the family trust and interests, if we indeed never even fellowship with the family except when we come with our hand out, we can hardly expect to claim privilege because of the family name.

Sometimes we worry about people abusing or misusing the name of the Lord. But, the name of Christ is its own safeguard. It is a spiritual power which no one can use unless he obtains it by living and acting in that name.

This explanation just barely touches the surface of what it means to pray in Christ's name. I pray that you will go deeper and search further to get into the very essence, nature, presence, and relation with Christ through the discovery of his name in your prayers and life.

> The saints in prayer appear as one
> In word and deed and mind;
> Where with the Father and the Son
> Sweet fellowship they find.

James Montgomery

CHAPTER SIX
IN HIS WILL:
The Holy Spirit

"Nor is prayer made by man alone:
   The Holy Spirit pleads;
And Jesus, on the eternal Throne,
   For sinners intercedes."

JAMES MONTGOMERY, *What Is Prayer?*

"And in His will is our peace."

DANTE ALIGHIERI, *Paradiso, III*

Now we come to the most difficult step in learning to pray in harmony with God. Believers do not have a hard time acknowledging the power of the heavenly Father. Neither do Christians have much difficulty in ascertaining the nature of the human Son. But, there are many problems in trying to know what the will of God is in matters which are not specifically dealt with in the Scriptures.

The third Person of the eternal Godhead, the Holy Spirit, provides the wisdom and activity to know and do God's will. God is one and in absolute harmony with himself. If we are to emulate that harmony in our praying, we need to relate to all three expressions of the triune God. We must pray in the power of the heavenly Father, in the name of the human Son, and in the will of the Holy Spirit.

First, we need to understand how the Spirit relates to

73

the Father and the Son in our prayer life, and then we will see how the Spirit actively participates in our praying. The eighth chapter of Romans contains three very distinct verses which deal with each of these three areas of the Spirit's ministry. You need to have your Bible open to that chapter as we study these passages together.

THE SPIRIT AND THE FATHER'S WILL

"And he that searcheth the hearts knows what the mind of the Spirit is, because he makes intercession for the saints according to the will of God" (Rom. 8:27). *The Living Bible* paraphrases this verse in the language of the harmony theme of our book: "And the Father who knows all hearts knows, of course, what the Spirit is saying as he pleads for us in harmony with God's own will."

The New English Bible reveals the intensity that should be felt in this verse: "God who searches our inmost being (remember our descriptions of primary prayer) knows what the Spirit means, because he pleads with God's people in God's own way."

That last translation may give a broader understanding of the term "God's will." You may have limited your idea of God's will to being a specific thing God wants to do, but it can also mean the general way in which God does everything. Will and way go hand in hand with God. He wills nothing that is contrary to his way.

It is also apparent from this verse that the knowledge of God's will is primarily a matter of the heart, or "our inmost being." One of the very first actions of the church was an almost verbatim fulfillment of this verse. After Jesus' ascension, his disciples met in the upper room to pray and organize. The first order of business was to designate someone to take Judas' place. Two men were nominated, Justus and Matthias. "And they prayed, and said, Thou, Lord, which knowest the hearts of all men, shew whether of these two thou hast chosen" (Acts 1:24).

Paul later wrote in Romans about God, who knows our hearts and reveals to us his own heart, that is, his will and way. The expression of God working in the human heart is known as the Holy Spirit.

The Holy Spirit knows the will of God because he *is* God. The same God known in creation as heavenly Father is known in the human heart as the Holy Spirit.

The Spirit in the human heart is not a special creation, addition, or gift from God. It is none other, and no less, than God himself. "Know ye not that ye are the temple of God, and that the Spirit of God dwelleth in you?" (1 Cor. 3:16).

This means that when the Holy Spirit is convicting our heart about God's will, we are dealing directly with God himself. When the Scripture says that the Holy Spirit makes intercession for us, this does not mean that a third party negotiates with God for us. It means, rather, that God has graciously allowed our hearts to know his heart through the communication of our spirit with his Spirit.

God takes the initiative in placing his Spirit within us. It is not something we have achieved, but have received. "I will put my Spirit within you, and cause you to walk in my statutes, and ye shall keep my judgments and do them" (Ezek. 36:27).

This is not simply the spirit of discernment or wisdom which the natural man exercises. The Christian has received a special internal presence of God's Spirit which communicates God's will in ways the world knows nothing about. "Even the Spirit of truth; whom the world cannot receive, because it seeth him not, neither knoweth him; but ye know him; for he dwelleth with you, and shall be in you" (John 14:17).

Neither is this merely your conscience at work. The conscience is the sense of "oughtness" and reflects what has been taught that ought to be done. Paul wrote to the Corinthians about eating meat that had been offered to idols, which was causing some of the new Christians to have guilty consciences. He reminded them that "there is only one God . . ." However, some Christians didn't realize this. All their lives they had been used to thinking of idols as alive, and believed that food offered to the idols was really being offered to actual gods. So when they ate such food it bothered them and hurt their tender consciences. The ideal state of the Christian is to have his natural sense of oughtness (conscience) instructed and inspired by the Holy Spirit. Paul presented exactly this case: "I say the truth in Christ, I lie not, my conscience also bearing me witness in the Holy Ghost" (Rom. 9:1).

When your sense of oughtness has been possessed by and enlightened by the Spirit of God, you will know how to pray about the will of God. Remember, though, that the Holy Spirit is one with the heavenly Father and will inspire and communicate only those requests which are in harmony with the revealed God of the Bible.

THE SPIRIT AND THE SON'S LIFE

Paul wrote: "It is Christ who died, and furthermore is also risen, who is even at the right hand of God, who also makes intercession for us" (Rom. 8:34). This may appear to contradict another verse, which stated that the Holy Spirit makes intercession for us (v. 27). This verse says that it is Christ who makes intercession at the right hand of God. How can these two verses be reconciled? The answer is very important in discovering how to pray in harmony with God.

The Holy Spirit knows the will of God because the Holy Spirit *is* God. It is also true that the Holy Spirit intercedes as Christ intercedes because the Holy Spirit and Christ are one. In the perfect harmony of the Godhead there is no essential difference in the three. They all represent in perfect harmony one God and one Lord.

The only life the Spirit can live in you is the life which the Son lived during his lifetime. Any other kind of life is not of the Spirit. The life of the Spirit is the continuous life of the Son.

The new life in which Christians share through grace by faith is a state of being "in the Spirit," a state in which the Spirit of God dwells in believers, as we see in Romans 8. The Spirit of God is also called the Spirit of Christ. "The Spirit of God dwell[s] in you. If any man have not the

Spirit of Christ, he is none of his" (v. 9). "And if Christ be in you . . . the Spirit is life because of righteousness" (v. 10). This is again equated with the "Spirit of him who raised up Jesus from the dead" (v. 11).

It is in the Spirit that the believer and the church are united to the Lord. Thus, the Spirit and Christ are both spoken of as the principle of new life.

The Holy Spirit is the "Spirit of Jesus Christ" (Phil. 1:19). Notice that the name Jesus has been added here. The Holy Spirit not only represents to your heart the Spirit of the eternal Christ; he also represents to your heart the life of the man Jesus of Nazareth.

Now, we come down to the heart of all this. The decisive test as to whether an inspiration is an authentic expression of the will of God is its comparison with the life of that man who embodied the essence of God on this earth for thirty-three years. The Holy Spirit will not inspire you to do anything or ask for anything which contradicts the life of Jesus as recorded in the Gospels.

On one occasion, Jesus was rejected by a Samaritan village. His disciples were indignant, and said, "Lord, wilt thou that we command fire to come down from heaven, and consume them?" But Jesus rebuked them and said, "Ye know not what manner of spirit ye are of. For the Son of man is not come to destroy men's lives but to save them" (Luke 9:54-56).

The disciples were ready to pray for fire to destroy their enemies, just itching to use this new power, and what better use than to wipe out those who rejected and humiliated them? But Jesus said they were not clear yet about the spirit behind the power. What was the spirit? It was the Spirit of the Son of man who had come to save lives, not destroy them.

Now, keeping that Scripture in mind, move across the centuries and continents to America engaged in its horrible Civil War. Christians were fighting Christians. Ministers were among the most fanatical on both sides. The churches played a major role in dividing the nation. Sermons were preached and public prayers composed specifically to incite the people to war. In the South, the noted theologian Robert Lewis Dabney called on God for a "retributive providence" which would demolish the North. In the North, the popular preacher Henry Ward Beecher prayed that the Southern leaders "be whirled aloft and plunged downward forever and ever in endless retribution." They sounded an awful lot like the disciples praying for fire to destroy their enemies, and not at all like the spirit of our Lord. Even great theologians sometimes pray and preach outside the Spirit of Christ.

In his second inaugural address, Abraham Lincoln seemed to more accurately represent the religious positions. "Both parties read the same Bible, and pray to the same God, and each invokes his aid against the other. The prayers of both could not be answered; that of neither has been answered fully."

Regardless of how much you may feel or think yourself to have the presence and power of the Holy Spirit, remember Jesus' statement to his disciples and ask yourself the question: "Do you know what manner of spirit you are of?"

THE SPIRIT AND THE SAINTS' PRAYERS

We have seen how the Spirit relates to the Father's will and the Son's life. But, how does he actually assist the believer in praying? Paul explained: "Likewise the Spirit also helpeth our infirmities: for we know not what we should pray for as we ought: but the Spirit itself maketh intercession for us with groanings which cannot be uttered" (Rom. 8:26).

Notice the first word of this verse, "Likewise," which refers back to the preceding words in verses 24 and 25: "Hope that is seen is not hope: for what a man seeth, why doth he yet hope for? But if we hope for that we see not, then we do with patience wait for it." Then, comes the word, "Likewise the Spirit also helps in our weaknesses."

The help of the Spirit in our praying is directly connected to our persevering in hope. There are so many times when we just could not go on hoping if it were not for that supernatural strength from the Spirit. How many times have you almost given up, and almost quit praying, but something inside you just wouldn't turn loose? Somehow you hung on until finally the answer came.

This is definitely one way the Spirit helps you in your praying—he gives you the staying power. When logic and experience tell you it is foolish to keep praying and hoping, a small steady fire burns deeply somewhere within, telling you to pray on and press on.

Another way the Spirit helps you in your praying is to encourage you that God knows your heart even when you yourself don't know what is the right thing to ask for. "We do not know what we should pray for as we ought."

Remember, this is the great apostle Paul writing. He who had such intimate fellowship with God and power in the Spirit admitted that he did not always know what to pray for. Just the knowledge that you are not alone in this dilemma should be an encouragement.

The real heart of this passage is the word *groan*. When we don't know what to pray for, "the Spirit itself makes intercession for us with *groanings* which cannot be uttered [or put into words]."

This was a very deliberate choice of words on Paul's part. It is just too close to two other occurrences of the same word to be a coincidence. In verse 21 and 22 he said that "the universe itself is to be freed from the shackles of mortality and enter upon the liberty and splendor of the children of God. Up to the present, we know, the whole created universe groans in all its parts as if in childbirth" (NEB).

Then, in verse 23 he continues, "Not only so, but even we, to whom the Spirit is given as firstfruits of the harvest to come, are groaning inwardly while we wait for God to make us his sons and set our whole body free."

The word *groan* implies a deep unutterable craving. You have seen people who are in a coma or deliriously ill, moaning or groaning. Although they are not conscious and able to articulate their needs, their body takes over and speaks for them. The groaning subsides when relief is sufficient.

An infant cannot talk, but it has needs and desires, and

expresses these through crying or groaning. It is not intelligent enough to know what is causing the pain, but it continues to wail until the pain is relieved. A deep craving for relief is sensed in the very nature of the wail.

Paul said that God's whole created universe is craving intently for its release from the shackles of mortality, reminiscent of slaves moaning in their chains. He said that redeemed man is also craving for total freedom. This deep craving of the universe and of redeemed man is a craving to be what God had originally created him to be before sin shackled him.

The groanings or moanings which the Spirit translates from our heart to the Father's heart are the cravings to become what God has created us to be. We are in binding shackles and unbearable pain in the contradiction of our flesh. Like the infant, we may not know what is causing the pain, but we groan for relief. The desparately ill person may have no idea what medicine to ask for, but his groanings attract the attention of the physician who knows what he needs. An infant does not know the reason for his discomfort and the accompanying cry, but a loving sensitive mother can tell what is wrong just by its particular cry.

Jesus said, "Blessed are they which do hunger and thirst after righteousness, for they shall be filled" (Matt. 5:6). Could this be something of what Paul meant? The deep hunger and thirst, the craving of the soul that goes so deep it cannot be expressed with words? Is this the groaning of the Spirit? If so, it is a craving for righteousness, not for things. This also parallels the thought about the universe and redeemed man craving to be what God had created him to be—what else in righteousness but this?

There is a deep hunger in your soul. Sometimes you try to satisfy it with things you believe will work. You even pray for some of those things. But the Spirit of God knows what the hunger is and what it will take to satisfy it. Do not hold back the groanings of your inmost being. Don't even hesitate to ask for what you think you need. But,

In His Will: The Holy Spirit

always keep in mind that the Spirit of God knows exactly what God's will is for meeting that need.

Now, you can begin to understand why Paul exhorts us to "pray at all times in the Spirit, with all prayer and supplication" (Eph. 6:18, RSV). Every prayer and every supplication must be in harmony with the Spirit by whom "we have access . . . unto the Father" (Eph. 2:18).

We return now to the symbol which represents a life of harmonious prayer. The circle with the inner circles is our PSM (Primary, Secondary, and Motive prayers in harmony with each other). Our PSM expresses itself in harmony with God, symbolized by a wide band of flowing revelation, a concept which will be more fully explained later.

PSM

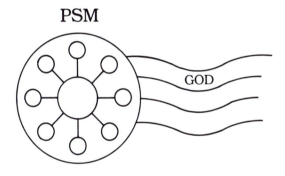

Peace of mind
read the Bible
Pray
do things for others
worship
attitude-open
seek counsel

PART 3

Pray in Harmony with Yourself

"How sweet the moonlight
sleeps upon this bank.
Here we will sit,
and let the sounds of music
Creep in our ears:
soft stillness and the night
Become the touches of sweet harmony.
Such harmony is in immortal souls;
But, whilst this muddy vesture of decay
Doth grossly close it in,
we cannot hear it."

SHAKESPEARE
The Merchant of Venice

"This above all:
to thine own self be true."

SHAKESPEARE
Hamlet

THERE is no true prayer without truth itself. It is impossible to communicate with God if you are holding back either facts or feelings. God knows your heart and he knows everything about your situation. You cannot deceive God. When you are less than completely honest, you are only deceiving yourself.

Approaching God with the attitude that you deserve what you are about to request is self-deceit. "For if a man thinks himself to be something, when he is nothing, he deceiveth himself" (Gal. 6:3).

Claiming the promises of the Bible without obeying the commands of the Bible is a serious form of spiritual deceit. "But be ye doers of the word, and not hearers only, deceiving your own selves" (James 1:22).

If we think that we do not need to ask God for anything because we have all that we need we are not being humbly honest with ourselves. "Because thou sayest, I am rich, and increased with goods, and have need of nothing; and knowest not that thou art wretched, and miserable, and poor, and blind, and naked" (Rev. 3:17).

The worst self-deceit of all is to deny that we are sinners in need of God's forgiveness and cleansing. "If we say that we have no sin, we deceive ourselves, and the truth is not in us" (1 John 1:8). There are many ways we can be dishonest with ourselves and therefore dishonest in our praying. Real prayer is an exercise in absolute honesty.

What does it mean to be honest with oneself? How can this honesty with self be integrated into effective praying?

One word answers both questions—harmony, going back to our basic premise of getting what we pray for through the principle of harmony. We have seen how our prayers need to be in harmony with each other, and we have studied how to pray in harmony with God. Now, we come to the personal issue of praying in harmony with ourselves.

Being true to ourselves means being in harmony with our basic nature. God gave you your basic nature, and he desires to see it reach its full potential. A true prayer, whether primary or secondary (what or how), must in some way help your God-given nature develop its potential.

There are many models we could use to study your basic nature or true self. The three I have chosen are biblical models which give a rather well-rounded concept of the real you at prayer. To pray in harmony with yourself, you need to pray as the image of God, as the child of God, and as the handiwork of God.

CHAPTER SEVEN
AS THE IMAGE OF GOD

"Let each man think himself an
act of God; his mind a thought,
his life a breath of God."

PHILIP JAMES BAILEY, *Festus*

Man was created in the image of God. This is our basic nature by creation (see Gen. 1:26ff.; 5:1; 9:6). There are some who say that the term "image of God" means that man is a creature whose nature does not originate from below (evolution), and is thereby distinguished from all other creatures.

There are others who believe that the "image of God" refers to man's self-conscious, self-determined personality, the free "I," the dignity of man as man.

Still others insist that the phrase says nothing at all about the nature of man, but merely about his power of dominion and his position of preeminence which he holds in the created world.

Regardless of what the Old Testament meant by the "image of God," it is clear that the New Testament presents the work of Jesus Christ as being redemption and reconciliation in order to renew and restore the divine image of man.

In the first place, Jesus Christ was the only perfect,

unmarred image of God. "He is the image of the invisible God, the firstborn of every creature" (Col. 1:15). Elsewhere Paul spoke of ". . . Christ, who is the image of God" (2 Cor. 4:4). The same idea is present in Paul's words: "For in him dwelleth all the fulness of the Godhead bodily" (Col. 2:9).

God's purpose in sending Christ was to recreate a new humanity which would be "conformed to the image of his Son" (Rom. 8:29). Those who have accepted Christ "have put on the new man [nature], which is renewed in knowledge after the image of him that created him" (Col. 3:10).

So, the human race was originally created in the image of God. Sin marred (some say destroyed) that image. Christ came to restore those who believe in him to that image relationship with God. Thus, by original creation and by Christ's recreation, you are made in the image of God. That is your basic nature.

Successful praying must be in harmony with your basic nature as the image of God. In order to understand how prayer relates to the image of God, there are two words you need to keep in mind—reflection and communication.

The word "image" is also used in the Bible to refer to the reflection one would see in a mirror. The very existence of a reflection depends on something else. It is an existence which points back or refers back to something else.

As the image of God, your existence is nothing in itself and is not intelligible within itself. Your ground of existence and knowledge is in God. "But we all . . . beholding as in a glass [mirror] the glory of the Lord, are changed into the same image from glory to glory, even as by the Spirit of the Lord" (2 Cor. 3:18).

The phrase "are being changed [transformed] into the same image" is a very important phrase in helping you to pray in harmony with God and yourself. This phrase implies that God is still working on man. When the Bible says that God made man in his own image, it does not mean that the process was over and done with in one fell swoop. God decided to make the creature man in his own image, and he is still at it.

As the Image of God

God produced the other creatures in a finished state; they are what they ought to be, and so they remain. But God has retained man within his workshop, within his hands. He does not simply make man and finish him. The creatures which have not been endowed with reason are turned out as finished articles. Man, however, develops on the basis of his decision and response to the divine call.

Prayer is at the very heart of man's decision and response to the divine call. In prayer man both responds to the call to be like God, and he asks God for those things which will assist him in developing the image of God in himself.

We have talked about primary prayer, the fundamental cry of your soul, your basic reason for living. Now, we put primary prayer alongside God's primary purpose. God's primary purpose in creation was to make you in the image of God. His primary purpose in recreation is to conform you to the image of his Son.

Be honest. Be true to yourself. Are your prayers in harmony with God's purpose to fashion you in his image? Are you praying in such a way as to be God's assistant in the workshop where he is hammering out his image in you? Can you sincerely say, Lord, I want this prayer request only if it will make me more like Jesus?

Praying in harmony with yourself means in harmony with your true spiritual self, the image of God, which is reflected completely and plainly in Jesus Christ.

The other word to keep in mind is communication. Just as the image of God is the divine reflection being developed in man, so also the image implies man's responsive communication to God.

This observation suggests that when God said, "Let us make man in our image," he may have been implying something like this: "We have finished all of creation. The earth is beautiful but mute. The animals are alive, but they cannot communicate with us. Now, let us make a creature with whom we can fellowship, one which will reflect back to us. Let us make man in our image (reflection-communication)."

God gave man his life, his existence, as the very image

of God. He did not, however, fling it at him as a finished article. He offered it to him through a call, so man must answer by accepting this special life from God's own hands.

In his answer, man "repeats" the original divine word. He does not create a word of his own, but of his own free will he gives back the divine word of creation, saying, "Yes, I am thine." Man answers God in believing, responsive love, accepting in grateful dependence his destiny to which God has called him.

So, whereas we first spoke of "image" and "reflection," now we speak of "word" and "answer." God has spoken, and man is invited, allowed, obliged to answer. Man is now faced with the responsibility of response, and God has provided the vehicle for response, the holy communication we call prayer.

Our God is a God who communicates. In limitless ways he has let himself be known to his creatures. His superlative communication has been through Jesus Christ. "God, who at sundry times and in divers manners spake in time past unto the fathers by the prophets, hath in these last days spoken unto us by his Son" (Heb. 1:1, 2).

Communication is the expression of an idea or intention in such a way as to relate compatibly with another intelligent being. When Jesus was given as God's superlative communication, he was identified as the Word. "In the beginning was the Word, and the Word was with God, and the Word was God. . . . And the Word was made flesh, and dwelt among us" (John 1:1, 14).

All interpersonal enterprises begin with words. People must communicate, exchange ideas, instruct, listen, and reason together in order to progress. The power and necessity of communication can never be overestimated.

In his divine grace God has seen fit to invite his creatures to communicate with him. Almighty God has given us the unbelievable privilege of entering into dialogue with the Creator of the universe: "Come now, and let us reason together, saith the Lord" (Isa. 1:18). When God created man in his image, he endowed him with the capacity to respond, to answer, to communicate with his Maker.

When Jesus tells us to pray, he is not introducing a new religious practice. He is encouraging us to claim our birthright. Humanity was born with the capacity and privilege of communicating with God. The new humanity in Christ is born again in the grace-faith communication between God and his "image."

To fail to pray is to deny your basic nature. An image both reflects and answers. As the image of God, it is your very nature to reflect the nature of God and to answer the call of God.

This means, of course, that the nature of your prayers should be such that they constitute a response to God's gracious call. Too many of our prayers are original ideas of expressing our desires, before we have reflected on God's desires. After reflecting on his desires, we should then respond by asking for those things which increase our conformity to his image and enhance our fellowship with his Spirit.

Try to evaluate some of your recent prayers. Have you been praying in harmony with your nature as the image of God? Are you asking for things which harmonize with God's creative purpose and process for you? Do your requests help or hinder the line of communication between you and God? Regardless of whether you have been getting your requests, has your fellowship with God deepened and grown?

Remember, prayer is not an issue between you and things, or between you and other people. Real prayer is a matter between you and God. An image is a reflection of the object it represents. As the image of God, you are to reflect him in all that you are and do. This is especially vital in the experience of prayer.

CHAPTER EIGHT
AS THE CHILD OF GOD

"The great man is he who does
not lose his child's-heart."

MENCIUS, *Works*, bk Ib

Your basic nature, by God's creation, is that you were made in the image of God. Your spiritual nature by God's grace is that you are a child of God. As you must pray in harmony with yourself as the image of God, so you must also pray in harmony with yourself as the child of God.

When Jesus taught us to pray, he underscored our relationship to God by telling us to pray, "Our Father . . ." However, this is not to be understood as a natural relationship for all men. The address "Our Father" is possible only because God is the Father of him who teaches his disciples to pray like this.

God has shown himself to be the Father in the coming of the Son, and those who recognize in their master the Son of his Father can and may also call God "Our Father." It is because of your connection with the Son that you have connection with the Father. You are a child of God not by natural birth, but by the new birth in Christ Jesus.

"He came to his own home, and his own people received him not. But to all who received him, who believed in his name, he gave power [the right] to become children of God" (John 1:11, 12, RSV).

All men are potentially the children of God, but the New Testament recognizes as actually such only those who have been begotten or born anew (John 3:3; 1 Peter 1:3; 2:2). They have been given birth by God (James 1:18). Paul often used the analogy of adoption to describe the believer's relation to the Father (Rom. 8:15; Gal. 4:5, 6).

The unmistakable truth is that one becomes a child of God by God's grace and love, and not by one's merits: "Behold, what manner of love the Father hath bestowed upon us, that we should be called the sons of God" (1 John 3:1).

The New Testament makes much of the spiritual heritage which the children of God receive. They are heirs of God and joint heirs with Christ (Rom. 8:17). They are even heirs of the hope of eternal life (Titus 3:7). They are heirs of God's promises and counsel (Heb. 6:17). This heirship, however, is always "through Christ" (Gal. 4:7).

As you claim your vast inheritance as a child of God, don't overlook that fabulous legacy—the right to pray "Our Father." You are not coming to a tight-fisted keeper of the treasury. You are not coming to an austere judge, or a remote monarch. You are coming to our Father, the Father of our Lord and Savior Jesus Christ who has made it possible for him to be our Father also.

In the previous chapter, we mentioned two words in connection with our nature as the image of God. Those words were *reflection* and *communication*. As we discuss our position as children of God, two important words are *trust* and *growth*.

Trust and *growth* are comprehensive words which span both the relationship and development of the child. They are also appropriate words to describe our prayer pilgrimage as children of God.

Trust is absolutely essential to the physical survival and emotional health of a child. Helpless and dependent, the child must trust others to care for him, and parents are the most natural and most common objects of trust.

The Bible abounds with exhortations for man to turn as a trusting child to God. "Trust in the Lord with all thine heart; and lean not unto thine own understanding. In all

As the Child of God

thy ways acknowledge him, and he shall direct thy paths" (Prov. 3:5, 6).

The whole concept of prayer is built on the premise of trust. Why in the world should we ever pray if we do not trust the Father with our prayers? And why would we need to pray unless we have found him alone to be sufficient?

"And such trust we have through Christ to God-ward: Not that we are sufficient of ourselves to think anything as of ourselves; but our sufficiency is from God" (2 Cor. 3:4-6).

Most books and sermons on prayer devote a great deal of time and space to the vital ingredient of faith. This is unquestionably an indispensable element of successful praying. Practically every prayer promise includes the requirement of faith.

"Have faith in God. Whosoever . . . shall not doubt in his heart, but shall believe that those things which he saith shall come to pass, he shall have whatsoever he saith. . . . believe that ye receive them, and ye shall have them" (Mark 11:22-24).

"Ask in faith, nothing wavering" (James 1:6).

"If thou canst believe, all things are possible to him that believeth" (Mark 9:23).

The evidence is overwhelming that prayer and faith must go together, and no discussion of prayer is adequate unless it considers this essential oneness. It is the child who teaches us the most about faith, and it is simple childlike faith which is required in prayer.

The matter of faith in prayer is the most perplexing of all to me. What is faith anyway? How do you know if you have enough? Why didn't you get what you really believed God was going to give you?

I do not have the answer to all these questions, and I think that more and deeper study needs to be done concerning the nature of faith. I think we should also be open to hear what others have learned in this area.

Andrew Murray associated faith with surrender and will. He wrote, "Faith is simply surrender; by faith I yield myself to the living God." But, he also developed an incisive study of Jesus' words to the blind man, "What wilt thou that I should do unto thee?" (Mark 10:51). He concludes that "Faith is nothing but the purpose of the will resting on God's word, and saying: I must have it. To believe truly is to will firmly."

I like this interpretation very much, but I still remember times when I willed firmly but did not receive. Does this mean I am not a man of faith, and should I feel guilty about it?

Harold Lindsell suggests that there are two kinds of faith, the gift of faith and the grace of faith. He explains that the gift of faith is one of the gifts of the Holy Spirit (1 Cor. 12:9). Some have this gift and some do not, just as some have the gift of preaching or administering and others do not. He points out that such a gift is from the Holy Spirit according to his sovereign good pleasure, and no one should feel special because he has it and no one should feel guilty because he doesn't.

The grace of faith, on the other hand, is available to all and belongs to all. It is based on some promise from the Word of God, and the absence of the grace of faith is sin. Noting these differences has prevented me from trying to force faith into my prayers when it did not come naturally.

I have heard some say that faith is believing that God *can* do something, not necessarily that he will. I have heard others say that real faith is believing not only that God can, but that he definitely *will*. This seems rather risky to me, especially when I cannot pinpoint a scriptural promise for a certain request.

My own personal posture of faith is very similar to that of Shadrach, Meshach, and Abednego, who were taunted about their God by Nebuchadnezzar as he was about to cast them into the fiery furnace. They said to the king: "O Nebuchadnezzar, we have no need to answer you in this matter. If it be so, our God whom we serve is able to deliver us from the burning fiery furnace; and he will deliver us out of your hand, O king. But if not, be it known to you, O king, that we will not serve your gods . . ." (Dan. 3:16-18, RSV).

Notice their progressive statement of faith: (1) our God is able to deliver us; (2) we believe he is going to deliver us; (3) but, if he does not, we will die serving and worshiping him anyway.

It may sound like weak faith to put in the "if he does not," but to me it is the real proof of genuine faith. The big question that every honest person tries to answer is, what will I do if he doesn't?

There seems to be an integral link between your faith (confidence) that something is going to happen and your faith (commitment) in God's sovereign grace. *Your confidence faith should be dependent on your commitment faith and not vice versa.* You believe that your prayers are answered because you believe in a God of grace and glory. You do not believe in a God of grace and glory because prayers are answered. It is very important to keep your faiths in order.

The child does not believe that he has a father because he gives him things. He believes that he will receive what he needs because he has a father.

The use of the word *trust* instead of the word *faith* to start this chapter was deliberate. While faith may be a difficult concept to get hold of, nearly everyone feels comfortable with the notion of trust. Even if you don't know what someone is going to do, or understand what they have done, you can still trust them.

This is what God calls us to do in our praying. As a child of God, trust your heavenly Father. Trust him to understand what you mean even if you don't know how to say it. Trust him to overlook your inadequacies and limitations. Trust him to love you more than you love yourself. Trust him to forgive you, and give you a clean slate. Trust him with time and circumstances. Trust him with people and problems. Trust him to do what is best, when it is best. When you don't get exactly what you asked for, keep trusting the Father, not the gift.

The second important word to keep in mind as a child of God is the word *growth.* The healthy, normal child grows and develops. He never outgrows his relationship to his parents. He is always their child, but he does not express his childishness at age forty the same way he did at age two.

"When I was a child, I spake as a child, I understood as a child, I thought as a child: but when I became a man, I put away childish things" (1 Cor. 13:11).

Your style of praying and your expectations in prayer should grow and mature along with the rest of your natural development. Is it possible that you are still saying "baby prayers" when you should be sitting in the high councils with God?

"You have been Christians a long time now, and you ought to be teaching others, but instead you have dropped back to the place where you need someone to teach you all over again the first principles in God's Word. You are like babies who can drink only milk, not old enough for solid food. And when a person is still living on milk it shows he isn't very far along in the Christian life, and doesn't know much about the difference between right and wrong. He is still a baby-Christian" (Heb. 5:12-13, TLB).

Are you still letting your parents tie your shoes and pick the clothes you wear? Do you still depend on them to provide every bite you eat and to arrange your daily schedule? Do you still run to their room during a thunderstorm? Does your father still have to hold your hand when you cross the street? Are you old enough to make responsible decisions and purchases?

I am not suggesting that God is not interested in the small events of our everyday life. The parent is always interested in his child's decisions and progress, but he knows that the child will never grow until he learns how to do some things for himself.

Also, I wonder what kind of conversations you have with your parents. Are you still talking about broken toys and potty training and the mean kids next door? One of the most delightful things we have enjoyed about our adult children is the way in which we can sit and talk with them about ideas, dreams, philosophies, or world needs. Don't you imagine that the heavenly Father would enjoy some adult conversation with some of his children occasionally?

What are some of the spiritually mature things that you could talk with God about in harmony with your position as his child? Some of the Scriptures which refer to us as his children also contain suggestions for prayer concerns: "Blessed are the peacemakers: for they shall be called the children of God" (Matt. 5:9). "[They] are the children of God, being the children of the resurrection" (Luke 20:36). "For as many as are led by the Spirit of God, they are the sons of God" (Rom. 8:14). "The Spirit itself beareth witness with our spirit, that we are the children of God" (Rom. 8:16). "In this the children of God are manifest . . . whosoever doeth not righteousness is not of God" (1 John 3:10).

Be candidly honest about your prayer habits. Is it possible that you are not getting what you are praying for because God is wanting you to move to a different level of spiritual concerns?

On the other hand, you may have moved to a much deeper level but you are still expecting God to give "quickie" answers like he did for your baby prayers. You may have quit praying for the child's tiny sailboat in the pond, and are now praying for a real ocean liner. That's all right, but remember that it takes a lot longer to build an ocean liner than it does a tiny sailboat.

Trust your Father and grow. As his child, it is your privilege and his joy to see you develop in harmony with his plan for your life.

CHAPTER NINE
AS THE HANDIWORK OF GOD

"What a piece of work is man!
How noble in reason! how infinite in
faculty! in form, in moving, how
express and admirable! in action
how like an angel! in apprehension
how like a god!"

SHAKESPEARE, *Hamlet, II*

"We all are the work of thy hand" (Isaiah 64:8).

"An honest man's the noblest work of God."

ALEXANDER POPE, *Epistle I*

You are called "the image of God" as an expression of God's original intention for you. You are called the child of God as an expression of God's redemptive relationship to you. You are called the handiwork of God as an expression of God's formative activity within you.

God is actively forming you, making you, developing you as his own handiwork. His work in you did not stop when you were converted. In fact, you were converted so that he might start his work within you.

"For it is by his grace you are saved, through trusting him; it is not your own doing. It is God's gift, not a reward for work done. There is nothing for anyone to boast of. For

101

Pray in Harmony with Yourself

we are God's handiwork, created in Christ Jesus to devote ourselves to the good deeds for which God has designed us" (Eph. 2:8-10, NEB).

If you are to pray in harmony with yourself as the handiwork of God, it will help you to know God's purpose and your part. In the chapter on the image of God we spoke of two important words—*reflection* and *communication*. In the chapter on the child of God we spoke of two more important words—*trust* and *growth*. Now, in this chapter on the handiwork of God, there are yet two more important words to keep in mind—*planned* and *productive*.

You are not an afterthought in God's scheme of things. You are a part of his great redemptive plan for mankind. Without you the puzzle of life would always have a missing piece. You are not a providential accident. God does not make mistakes. Human beings make mistakes and have terrible accidents, but that is not God's way.

We have to have this sense of a planned and purposeful existence in order to pray in harmony with God's design. We should examine again the Scriptures, which assure us of God's plan for us.

The Ephesians passage quoted above mentions that "for which God has designed us." The King James Version reads, "which God hath before ordained that we should walk in them." The Living Bible gives it vividly, "and long ages ago he planned that we should spend these lives in helping others."

The same word is variously translated as designed, ordained, and planned. The idea is essentially the same. God has a plan for you. One of the main objects of prayer is to discover that plan. Getting what you pray for should first mean discovering what God wants with your life.

Your first step in discovering God's plan for your life is recognizing God's sovereignty over all life. He may need to send you to the potter's house as he did Jeremiah, where the prophet was reminded of God's sovereignty: "So he made it again another vessel, as seemed good to the potter to make it. Then the word of the Lord came to me, saying, . . . Behold, as the clay is in the potter's hand, so are ye in mine hand" (Jer. 18:4, 6).

Remembering that you are the handiwork of God, look at that phrase again: "as seemed good to the potter to make it" then notice all the wonderful gifts of the Spirit mentioned by Paul (1 Cor. 12), which God uses to fashion us as his handiwork. Don't overlook the most significant note of all, "the same Spirit works all these things, distributing to each one individually as he wills" (1 Cor. 12:11, NASB).

God knows who needs which gift and he decides, as the potter decides, which vessel will serve what purpose. To pray in harmony with God's handiwork is to pray for God to reveal his sovereign will for your life.

God is sovereign in what he gives. Paul wrote, "And he gave some, apostles; and some, prophets; and some, evangelists; and some, pastors and teachers" (Eph. 4:11). If this is really true, if people have certain of these gifts because God has ordained and decreed that they should have them, you and I must not play God with other people's lives and ministries.

I have known church members who were determined to make their pastor more evangelistic even though the man was doing an outstanding job of pastoring, his obviously God-given ministry. I have seen good people frustrated and guilt-ridden by trying to be all that others expected. The Scripture does not say that God would give every person every gift, but to each as he sees best.

This passage should be taken at face value. God does the calling and the giving of gifts. We should not try to impose our idea of ministry on someone else, or even on ourselves. We should not pray that God will make our pastor or teacher more evangelistic, or pray that God will make an evangelist more scholarly. We should pray that each will find and fulfill his own calling and develop his own gift.

This passage implies that the primary calling of God is to a certain ministry, not to a certain place. I believe that God definitely may give you a secondary calling, for example, which class he wants you to teach. But the primary calling is to teach in the first place.

Many Christians chase rainbows all their lives, thinking that they can be the big success in just the right place. There is a certain amount of truth to this. The right people and the right places do need to get together. But usually the first order of business is to ascertain *what* you are supposed to be, not *where* you are to be.

The Scripture does not say that God gave some to Africa and some to America and some to China. That does happen, and it will happen in the right order. But, first you must read, "He gave some apostles, and some prophets, and some evangelists, and some pastors and teachers." Don't start praying about *where* God wants you to be until he has answered your prayer about *what* he wants you to be.

The second important word in this chapter is *productive*. Just as surely as God has a plan for your life, he wants it to be a productive plan. Understanding and fulfilling this purpose of God is an essential element of the successful prayer life. We are not having to force this into an artificial setting for the purpose of this book. Jesus plainly tied all three together—the planned life, the productive life, and the praying life:

"You did not choose Me, but I chose you, and appointed you, that you should go and bear fruit, and that your fruit should remain, that whatever you ask the Father in My name, He may give to you" (John 15:16, NASB).

Paul said that we are married to Christ for the purpose of bringing forth fruit unto God (Rom. 7:4). He described this as the fruits of righteousness unto the glory of God (Phil. 1:11). He emphasized that we are pleasing unto God when we are "being fruitful in every good work" (Col. 1:10).

That last passage cited is a key statement to praying in harmony with yourself as God's handiwork. The productive fruit of your life is not simply to excel at your profession or to acquire through your skills. That is the successful productivity of the world. When you have gained wealth, position, and power, the world sees you as a healthy, productive example for society.

This is not the same pattern of productivity for the Christian. When two of Jesus' disciples asked him for successful positions, he said to them, "Ye know that they which are accounted to rule over the Gentiles exercise lordship over them; and their great ones exercise authority upon them. But so shall it not be among you; but whosoever will be great among you shall be your minister. And whosoever of you will be the chiefest, shall be servant of all" (Mark 10:42-44).

Christ's standard for a productive, successful career is the model of servanthood. God is not making you (his handiwork) for the sake of your own success. He is fashioning you so that you will be able to serve others. Remember the Ephesian text: "He planned that we should spend these lives in helping others."

I think it is certainly proper for you to pray for success in your work, and for development of your skills. The secret is the motive behind the prayer. Are you praying for that success and development so that you will be better equipped to serve others in the name of Christ?

There is another facet of productivity which you need to keep in mind as you pray, and this is also connected to the sovereign plan of God for your life. It is the design of the Creator of the universe that things should produce their own kind.

"And God said, Let the earth bring forth grass, the herb yielding seed, and the fruit tree yielding fruit after its kind, whose seed is in itself. . . . And God said, Let the earth bring forth the living creature after his kind, cattle, and creeping thing, and beast of the earth after its kind" (Gen. 1:11, 24).

If you pray in harmony with your own nature, your nature as God has made you, according to his sovereign will, you must pray for fruit which comes naturally from its own seed-kind.

If an apple tree could pray, its duty would be to pray for a good crop of apples. Apple trees should not pray for a harvest of acorns, and oak trees should not pray for a harvest of apples.

It was proper for Shakespeare to pray to write great plays, and for Columbus to pray to discover new worlds, and for Edison to pray to invent the light bulb and phonograph. But, wouldn't it have been absurd for Edison to pray to write *Hamlet*, or for Shakespeare to pray to invent the phonograph?

I love great music and accord it its rightful place in worship. But I am not at all musical. But when I was younger I used to fantasize about leading a symphony orchestra or a great choir. I even visualized myself as a great soloist. But, God simply did not give me any ability in that direction. Wouldn't it be inconsistent with the order of the Creator for me to pray for fruit where there is no seed whatsoever?

But, you ask, don't I believe in miracles? Don't I believe that God could supernaturally give me a musical ear and a melodious voice? I believe in a God who can do anything he wants to; with God nothing is impossible. But, I think he has already made it clear to me that he doesn't want me to be a musician, or he surely would have planted a little seed of it somewhere in me. On the other hand, there are thousands of people who do have musical talent with which they could bless so many lives if they would only develop what God has given them.

Doesn't it make more sense for me to pray for God to help me develop and produce according to my own kind of seed than to be trying to get a miraculuous shot of what he has already given naturally to someone else?

Harmony! That's the word. Get in harmony with yourself. Be honest with yourself about what God has done, is doing, and can do in your life. You are the handiwork of God, but he needs your cooperation in completing the project. "For we are God's fellow workers; you are God's field, you are God's building" (1 Cor. 3:9, NIV).

The Sunday school teacher was coaching Johnny to understand that all things come from God. "And God made the flowers, didn't he, Johnny?"

"Yes, ma'am."

"And God made the birds, didn't he, Johnny?"

"Yes, ma'am."

"And God made you, didn't he, Johnny?"

"Well, ma'am, he made something about this big [holding his hands about eighteen inches apart], but *I* grew the rest of me."

That's right, Johnny. You are God's fellow worker. You are his handiwork, something grand and beautiful he is making. And he has given you the wonderful privilege and awesome responsibility of being a partner with him in the project.

Pray in harmony with God's sovereign plan for your life, and pray in harmony with the fruit of servanthood. You will discover that you are not only talking with God; you are working alongside God.

This brings us to another symbol of praying in harmony. We are now ready to add one more part to the symbol. The harmonious circles represent our PSM (Primary, Secondary, and Motive prayers). The first flowing band represents praying in harmony with God. Now we add the second band which represents praying in harmony with self and flows together with being in harmony with God.

PSM

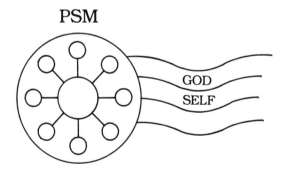

PART 4

Pray in Harmony with Nature

"From harmony,
from heavenly harmony,
This universal frame began:
From harmony to harmony
Through all the compass
of the notes it ran,
The diapason closing full in man."

JOHN DRYDEN
A Song for St. Cecilia's Day

YOU are a vital part of God's world. In fact you are the magnificent climax of his creation symphony, "The diapason closing full in man."

But, you must never forget that you *are* a part of nature, even though its noblest part. You belong to this universe as sure as the trees or water belong to it. In fact, the biblical account of creation says that man came from the very dust of the ground. These picturesque passages give the inseparable link between God, man, and nature:

"And the Lord God formed man of the dust of the ground, and breathed into his nostrils the breath of life; and man became a living soul. And the Lord God planted a garden eastward in Eden; and there he put the man whom he had formed" (Gen. 2:7, 8).

There they are, together from the very beginning—God, man, and nature, working in beautiful harmony. Your prayer life is your God-given opportunity to continue that harmony. We have seen how you are to pray in harmony with God, and in harmony with yourself, and now we will try to understand how you can pray in harmony with nature.

If you were created within nature, and you are sustained by the life-support systems of nature, it seems reasonable that your most satisfactory prayer life will be one that harmonizes with the laws of nature to which you yourself are subject.

I believe that many people do not get what they pray for because they are determined to control or change nature. They have not learned the exciting power of coordinating God's natural laws through harmonious prayer.

Ivan Turgenev once said, "Whatever a man prays for, he prays for a miracle. Every prayer reduces itself to this: Great God, grant that twice two be not four."

Many people do pray that way, but I reject his generalization that all prayer is for God to change the laws of nature. There are many sincere Christians who pray daily to know how to serve God better within the natural laws of this created world of his. They do not ask God to change his created order; they ask for the best of all possibilities within that order. They do not pray for evil to vanish from the earth; they pray for right to prevail. They do not pray to be forever free from suffering; they pray for strength to endure.

We are talking about praying in harmony with nature in such a way as to participate with God in accomplishing his purposes on earth. We are talking about how you can become a partner with God in the marvelous things he wants to do for his people while they are still bound by the laws of nature.

In order to pray like this in harmony with nature, you need to have a clear idea of what kind of world your God has created. I see God's world as an orderly world, a benevolent world, and a redemptive world. From these three perspectives, we will look at the relationship between your prayers and God's world.

CHAPTER TEN
AN ORDERLY WORLD

"Here hills and vales, the woodland and
  the plain.
Here earth and water seem to strive again,
Not chaos-like together crushed and bruised,
But, as the world, harmoniously confused:
Where order in variety we see,
And where, though all things differ, all agree."

ALEXANDER POPE, *Windsor Forest*

When I was a young boy, hoeing cotton in West Texas, I decided one day to test the promises of the Bible concerning prayer. I remember that Jesus had said that if a person really believed, without any doubt in his heart, he could cast a mountain into the sea by just commanding it.

So, I closed my eyes and prayed as fervently as I knew how with all the faith I had in my young heart, and asked that when I opened my eyes, all the weeds in that field would be gone. Sure enough, when I opened my eyes every single weed was still there. In fact, it looked like even more.

Many years later, I was pastoring a church in East Texas and was nearing the completion on my work for the Ph.D. at Baylor University. I was scheduled for the qualifying exam in French which would complete all my language requirements. I knew the nature of the exam; I would be given an article from a French theological journal and would have to translate it with a 90 percent proficiency in a given period of time.

With the same believing heart which had asked for the weeds to disappear, I prayed again. This time I did not pray for God to work any magic or to give me any supernatural knowledge I had not already acquired through study. I did not even pray the overall prayer that I would pass. I asked for one particular thing. Theology is such a "wordy" subject that it is sometimes difficult to understand even in English. So I prayed that I would be given an article that would be easily understood if it were in English. I was willing to do my part on the translation work. Not only did I get such an article, but I received a 97 percent rating, and became so interested in the subject matter of the article that I went immediately to the library to do further reading on it—in English!

What was the difference between these two prayer experiences of mine? I think there were two basic issues involved: God's world order and my personal growth. In the first prayer I was asking God to change the laws of nature for my benefit. At first my young faith was disappointed, but I came to realize that a positive answer to that prayer would have hindered the mature process of growth through responsibility.

In the later prayer I did not ask God to rearrange anything in the natural order. I did not even ask him to tell me the meaning of a single word I did not already know. I asked only that I would have the opportunity to exercise my ability freely and adequately. The results added to my spiritual growth and my intellectual knowledge.

I think you can develop a more consistently successful prayer life by praying in harmony with those same two principles: God's world order and your own spiritual growth. In fact, you need to think of these two principles as compatible and inseparable.

Personal life could not develop except in a stable environment. How could you possibly make decisions and mature if you had no law-abiding stability in your world?

An Orderly World

How could people know how to protect themselves from certain kinds of storms if those storms were not predictable in their natural course?

Fire must burn a child when he touches it or he will never learn to avoid it. A wooden beam must strike in painful force, or you will never learn to dodge it. The law of gravity cannot be suspended when a Christian falls from a tall building, or safety measures would be totally neglected (or there would be wholesale conversions to Christianity).

Jesus rejected the temptation to jump off the temple and be miraculously saved from injury. He also rejected the temptation to turn stones into bread. His kingdom would not be built on magic for the sake of magic.

He did, of course, perform many miracles which I accept as true accounts of his authentic divinity. Even then, however, he seemed to work within natural order. Water turned into wine still remains the basic liquid state. The five thousand are fed from loaves and fish, the regular food for human beings. When the disciples caught a great multitude of fish at Jesus' command, the net broke, a simple testimony to the fact that even miracles have to put up with nature's laws.

When Jesus was conceived of the Holy Ghost within the virgin Mary, the young woman still went through the normal nine months of pregnancy and a normal birth. C. S. Lewis said, "The divine art of miracle is not an art of suspending the pattern to which events conform but of feeding new events into that pattern. A miracle is emphatically not an event without cause or without results. Its cause is the activity of God; its results follow according to natural law. Miraculous wine will intoxicate, miraculous bread will be digested, miraculous conception will lead to pregnancy. Miracles, if they occur, must, like all events, be revelations of the total harmony of all that exists."

Once again we encounter the theme word of our book—harmony! Answered prayer, even so drastic as to be termed a miracle, still reveals itself as a part of God's harmonious world. A vital part of growing up is to realize that certain things in this world are not going to change just for you. A vital step in spiritual growth is to realize that the constancy of God's creation is your friend, not your enemy. Getting in step with nature may help you get in step with God's purpose.

"One generation passeth away, and another generation cometh: but the earth abideth for ever. The sun also ariseth, and the sun goeth down, and hasteth to his place where he arose. The wind goeth toward the south, and turneth about unto the north; it whirleth about continually, and the wind returneth again according to his circuits. All the rivers run into the sea; yet the sea is not full; unto the place from whence the rivers come, thither they return again. All things are full of labour; man cannot utter it: the eye is not satisfied with seeing, nor the ear filled with hearing" (Eccl. 1:4-8).

Is this fatalism, which leaves no room for the power of prayer? Not at all. In fact, I don't see how you can pray at all unless you believe in a God who is dependable as well as all-powerful. The magnificent hymn, Psalm 104, is devoted to the creative work and sustaining providence of God, and helps us understand how God works in and through his natural laws.

When the Israelites were crossing the wilderness, they were destitute and hungry. When Moses took the matter to God in prayer, God did not change the physical structure of their bodies so that they could live unlimited days without food. Instead, he provided a desert food (manna) and swarms of quail for them to eat. It was an answer to prayer, but in harmony with his existing laws of nature.

No, I do not agree with Ivan Turgenev that all prayer is asking God that two plus two not equal four. On the contrary, I think that mature prayer consists of asking God how we can work with him to insure that the right two and two get together to produce the perfect four.

If you receive a letter which you fear has bad news in it, I do not think you can possibly change the contents of that letter you hold in your hand regardless of how hard you pray. I do think, however, that you may have a decided influence on the contents of that letter by something you say or do or pray before the letter is sent. I also believe that you can pray successfully for God to give you the strength and wisdom you will need to handle the news if it is bad.

In one of our former pastorates, a woman in our church asked my wife and me to come to her house to pray with her about an urgent matter. When we got there, she told us that the doctors suspected that she had cancer, and that she was going to a large clinic the next day to find out for sure. She begged us to claim God's power and promise and to pray that the doctors would find no cancer when she got there.

I told her that we were deeply concerned and would be praying constantly for her, but that I could not pray the prayer she was asking. I said, "You either do or you don't have a malignancy in your body at this moment. My praying cannot change that fact. But I will pray that if you do have it, the doctors will find it, that you will have the best care possible, and that you will return to us to live a happy and fruitful life."

The tests were positive. She did have cancer, and God did answer the prayers we prayed for her. That was several years ago and she is still living a busy and productive life.

One of our greatest hindrances to prayer is the mistaken belief that prayer is neither needed nor heeded unless it calls for some extraordinary act of God. Our problem is that we have such a difficult time conceding that an ordinary act can be just as much the work of God as the extraordinary. The solution to our problem is to believe in a God great enough and wise enough to act in the ordinary or extraordinary way as he sees best.

I believe that God works in many ways, his will to accomplish and his wonders to perform. Some of these ways are miraculous and very limited in number. Others are marvelous and happen innumerable times every day. Miraculous and marvelous are two different things.

In my illness and healing, I believe God was at work, marvelously but not miraculously. It was not miraculous (the introduction of a new element into the physical world) when my discs ruptured and were repaired by surgery and modern medicine. Well-meaning friends tried to get me to testify that God miraculously healed me from MS. But the truth is that I never did have MS, only a very messed up back. My healing was not miraculous, but it certainly was marvelous.

It was marvelous that we were in the right place at the right time to receive the proper treatment, and I believe that God was in that. It was marvelous that our financial needs were met in an unexpected way, and I believe God led in that. It was marvelous that our family and our work and our attitude and our church were all sustained through those many months, and I believe God was in all of that. It was marvelous that each need was met as it arose, that wisdom was given when decisions had to be made, that people and events all synchronized in a plan that, now, in retrospect, was clearly God's doing.

But in all this doing of marvelous things, we saw the Lord working through natural processes, through his church, through people who made themselves available by training and resources. Yes, a thousand times, yes, God was working, and by doing so was answering many prayers. But we must not give instructions to God as to *how* he will answer prayers. What we must do is to believe implicitly in *him*, not the process. We must be committed to his will, not to magical powers.

Does this leave room for the miraculous to happen in today's world? Absolutely! Notice that I said we must believe in God, not the process. In our chapter on the power of God I emphasized that nothing is impossible with God, but I also insisted that true power accomplishes purpose, rather than exhibiting brute force.

God is able to break into nature with any new activity (what we call miracle) any time he chooses. There are many unexplained events which fit into this category. There are countless experiences of healing which defy medical explanation. Perhaps these were miraculous, the introduction of a new element. Perhaps they were marvelous, the synchronizing of existing elements in the perfect harmony necessary for healing.

An Orderly World

I am not limiting God in this chapter about an orderly world. This is God's world, and I believe completely in his absolute authority and power. I am trying to encourage you in your praying by pointing out that God can answer your prayers through ordinary as well as extraordinary acts. Regardless of his method, it is still God at work.

You do not have to be a miracle worker in order to do God's will and to be successful in your prayer life. We read that "John did no miracle, but all things that John spake of this man were true" (John 10:41). The real credentials of John the Baptist consisted of his true and faithful testimony concerning Christ, not his ability to perform miracles.

When you look at other passages about John, this one becomes even more remarkable. John's birth was attended by very extraordinary events. His preaching was unusually powerful, and his popularity rivaled that of Jesus. He had the singular privilege of being selected to baptize Jesus himself. His martyrdom is still studied as a classic of courage and integrity. He had disciples who continued unto the ministry of Paul and as far away as Ephesus. He was the last of the great line of Old Testament prophets, and the first New Testament proclaimer of the Kingdom of God. Jesus Christ said of him, "Verily I say unto you, Among them that are born of women there hath not risen a greater than John the Baptist" (Matt. 11:11). He went on to say that John's ministry was the beginning of a new age for the kingdom (Matt. 11:12, 13), and that he was the "Elijah" whom Malachi had said would come heralding the arrival of the Messiah (Matt. 11:14).

After reflecting on all those great accomplishments and accolades for John the Baptist, remember that "John did no miracle." Some men are chosen by God to be the instruments of his works of wonder and some are chosen for other purposes. For all his greatness (and Jesus said he was the greatest) John was not a miracle worker. God works through just plain people like you, and John, and me, who may never cause a miracle in the technical sense of that word, but who are daily partners with God in the work of the Kingdom of God on earth.

Don't let someone discourage you and hinder your prayers by suggesting that you don't have enough faith because you don't get miraculous results. Faith is an indispensable part of prayer, but your faith is to be in God, not in methods. Pray believing that God is in control of his orderly world, and that by praying and working in harmony with his will, you can be a key to power and a channel of blessing.

Remember Tennyson's words, "More things are wrought by prayer than this world dreams of. Wherefore, let thy voice rise like a fountain for me night and day." What may seem to be a natural event to us may, in fact, be the working of God in answer to some humble prayer. Let your voice "rise like a fountain night and day," and be available as God's means of bringing his will to fulfillment in your part of his world.

CHAPTER ELEVEN
A BENEVOLENT WORLD

"The year's at the spring
And day's at the morn;
Morning's at seven;
The hillside's dew-pearled;
The lark's on the wing;
The snail's on the thorn:
God's in his heaven—
All's right with the world."

ROBERT BROWNING, *Pippa Passes*

To pray in harmony with nature you must have an abiding conviction that God's world is a good world. If you see the world as evil or hostile, you will naturally want to change it or fight it. If you see it as inherently benevolent and friendly, you will want to know how to participate in helping the world achieve its highest good.

Because there is so much heartache and evil in the world, we are prone to indict the world itself as being the cause of all our hurts. Since God is the Creator of the world, the indictment ultimately must rest on him. And that is where we have difficulty in praying. How can we pray in faith and hope to a God who has created such a faithless and hopeless world?

Well, God didn't create that kind of a world. God created

a good world. The Genesis account points out the goodness of creation.

"And God called the dry land Earth; and the gathering together of the waters called he Seas: and God saw that it was good" (Gen. 1:10). "And God made two great lights . . . to rule over the day and over the night, and to divide the light from the darkness: and God saw that it was good" (Gen. 1:16-18). "And God created . . . every living creature that moveth . . . and God saw that it was good" (Gen. 1:21). "And God made the beast after his kind . . . and everything that creepeth upon the earth after his kind: and God saw that it was good" (Gen. 1:25). "And God saw everything that he had made, and behold it was very good" (Gen. 1:31). This last verse was given even after the creation of man (vv. 26-28). Yes, even man who fell into sin was originally considered "very good."

Although Paul told Timothy that the love of money is the root of all evil, originally even the gold of man's first home was seen as good: "And the gold of that land is good" (Gen. 2:12). God's creation was good. His world is a benevolent world. His intentions and plans were for a harmonious world with happy mankind at its center.

The very reason why the world has become a place of sorrow and horror is because man got out of harmony with God and his world. He disobeyed and partook of "forbidden fruit" in God's world. The reason for continuing disaster and tragedy in the world is the same. Man continues to live and work out of harmony with God and his creation.

Man's sin brought the curse of "thorns and thistles" to the earth and the curse of sorrow and death to himself (Gen. 3:17-19). The Christian message of hope is that God will one day liberate all of creation from this curse.

"For on that day thorns and thistles, sin, death, and decay—the things that overcome the world against its will at God's command—will all disappear, and the world around us will share in the glorious freedom from sin which God's children enjoy. For we know that even the things of nature, like animals and plants, suffer in sickness and death as they await this great event" (Rom. 8:20-22, TLB).

Notice that this passage is from the same setting in Romans which speaks of creation "groaning" for its release. This passage is also preceded by a familiar word of hope about suffering: "For I consider all that we suffer in this present life is nothing to be compared with the glory which by-and-by is to be uncovered for us. For all nature is expectantly waiting for the unveiling of the sons of God. For nature did not of its own accord give up in failure; it was for the sake of Him who let it thus be given up, in the hope that even nature itself might finally be set free from its bondage of decay, so as to share the glorious freedom of God's children. Yes, we know that all nature has gone on groaning in agony together till the present moment" (Rom. 8:18-22, WMS).

In summary: (1) God's original creation was good; (2) man's sin brought disorder into the world; (3) creation and redeemed mankind eagerly await release from the bondage imposed by sin; (4) and, in the meantime, all things continue to work together for good to those who love God (Rom. 8:28).

The "meantime" is where you and I are, and it is the arena for our faith and prayer activity. We are still in a world suffering from sin's result, and it is the only world we will have until Christ returns with the "new heaven and new earth."

But, God assures us that even in this meantime all things work together for good for those who love the Lord. This sounds like a hollow promise to those who have had tragedy and sorrow. All things that have happened to believers and lovers of God have not been good. Bad things do happen to good people.

Look at the promise again. It does not say that all things that happen to God's people are good. It says that all things—the good and the bad—*work together* for the eventual good. The dark threads must be woven with the golden threads to produce the divine design on God's tapestry for your life.

The next verse explains: "For whom he did foreknow, he did also predestinate to be conformed to the image of his Son" (Rom. 8:29). We are back again to the primary purpose of God, that we might be conformed to the image of Christ. Paul's argument was that predestination is related to God's goal for the Christian. His intention (predestination or primary purpose) for those whom he knew would accept Christ is for them to be conformed to his image, to become like Christ.

Your concern should not be about the theological confusion over God's foreknowledge, predestination, and election. As a Christian, your reaction should be: "God's plan for me all along (predestined) is that I should become like Jesus. In this imperfect, sin-cursed world everything that happens to me, good and bad, is working toward that end, to make me more like Jesus."

Your part in the enterprise is to pray creatively and openly to be a part of the unfolding good in God's plan. Remember, that right in the middle of this weighty discussion in Romans is the assurance that "the Spirit also helps us in our present limitations. For example, we do not know how to pray worthily, but his Spirit within us is actually praying for us in those agonizing longings which cannot find words. He who knows the heart's secrets understands the Spirit's intention as he prays according to God's will for those who love him" (Rom. 8:26, 27, PHIL).

To give added assurance that this is a meantime in which we can discover God's goodness and grace, Paul added, "What shall we then say to these things? If God be for us, who can be against us?" (Rom. 8:31).

Then follow the words of assurance: "Who shall separate us from the love of Christ? Shall tribulation, or distress, or persecution, or famine, or nakedness, or peril, or sword? As it is written, for thy sake we are killed all the day long; we are accounted as sheep for the slaughter. Nay, in all these things we are more than conquerors through him that loved us. For I am persuaded, that neither death, nor life, nor angels, nor principalities, nor powers, nor things present, nor things to come, nor height, nor depth, nor any other creature, shall be able to separate us from the love of God, which is in Christ Jesus our Lord" (Rom. 8:35-38).

If nothing can separate you from the love of God, regardless of how bad or tragic or evil, then this is indeed a good world. God is still on his throne!

Thus you can pray believing that good will triumph. You can pray expectantly, on tip-toe as it were, eagerly looking to see what God is going to bring out of this situation.

You can pray gratefully, realizing that God has given us a world which contains the resources for our needs.

Even though this world is stained with sin, there are still within it the essential provisions for conquering disease, securing peace, relieving poverty, and advancing civilization.

Man, however, will not always avail himself of those provisions, or he may pervert them to ungodly uses, and they will become destructive forces. But this is the perversion of man, not the provision of God. It was God who placed the iron ore in the earth for man's provision, but it is man who decides whether he will make a sword or a plow with the iron. If man ignores the belching warning of the volcano and builds his village too close to the mountain, he cannot accuse God of being evil or unprotective when the lava flows down.

The provisions of God will be consistent with his nature: mercy, truth, and justice. When the provisions appear as otherwise they have either been misunderstood or misused by man. We may not be able to know everything about God, but that which we do know bears the stamp of God in his mercy and truth and justice.

In his disposition of love toward man, God provides that which he needs, sometimes centuries before it is needed or discovered. Wallace Hamilton once wrote, "Think how the Creator has waited long centuries of time for the mind of man to open, to break through, and to learn even a little about the hidden mystery of creation. All these powerful energies here—half-concealed, waiting for someone's seeing eye and hearing ear." Emerson once hinted that they could have had electricity in the Garden of Eden. It was here from the beginning of time, waiting.

Uranium has been here all along, hidden in the rocks, to be discovered and utilized only in this, the nuclear age. Thousands of years before man began to use them, coal and oil existed in abundance. Nature had been storing up man's cellar with fire and fuel for his use, but for generations he shivered in his cold, damp houses, not knowing what was under his feet. Who knows what vast secrets of the universe are yet unlocked, what provisions of God are yet undiscovered?

In his autobiography *From Pagan to Christian*, Lin Yutang said, "If I were God, and therefore a master chemist and physicist, I would be extremely interested in seeing how the chemists and astronomers and biologists on earth proceed to unlock my secrets. I would, of course, remain silent and give no help. But I would be very interested in watching their discoveries, giving them perhaps a century or two to pry open my secrets and think them over and work them out."

Does one have to be a scientist to discover God's provisions? Are there special locations in the earth where one must go to pry open his secrets? Not at all. As Joseph Henry, the American physicist, said, "The seeds of great discoveries are constantly floating around us, but they only take root in minds well prepared to receive them."

This, then, is the key to opening the doors of providential provisions; a mind prepared to receive them. A mind and attitude that expect great and good things from a great and good God. A mind that thinks God is a provider who knows well in advance our needs. A mind that is capable of seeing the parallel between the physical world and the spiritual world, because the former is but the shadow of the latter. A mind and heart and soul that are willing to penetrate deeply into the essential nature of this created world, and into the attributes of the God who created it and ordained the nature of its laws.

Pray for God to enable you and others to use the provisions of his benevolent world for ministries of service which conform to the image of his dear Son. If you will really pray this way in harmony with God's benevolent plans through nature, you will be surprised how much you will get what you pray for.

Pray with an awareness of neutrality in the "things" of the world. Paul said, "I know, and am persuaded by the Lord Jesus, that there is nothing unclean of itself" (Rom. 14:14). In your mental preparation for prayer, position yourself as though you are in the middle. A vote has been cast for this "thing" to be used as evil, and a vote has been cast for it to be an instrument of good. You must cast the deciding, tie-breaking vote. Your life and prayers may determine what happens to this small part of God's world.

Nuclear power exists in many forms in the world today. The neutron bomb is a potential catalyst of horror, bringing death and suffering to millions. But nuclear medicine units are now saving lives in hospitals throughout the world. What man does with nuclear power determines whether it is good or evil. Who knows but what the power of prayer will eventually decide the destiny of this great force?

Pray also with a dedication to good beginnings rather than to good endings. Too many of us start out wrong and then pray for God to get us out of a jam we got ourselves into. Good endings are nearly always dependent on good beginnings. My students used to ask me if I thought it was all right to pray before an exam. I would answer, "Certainly you should pray before an exam—about six weeks before. Pray for God to help you keep your priorities in order and to do your very best in preparation." Don't destroy your health with bad habits and harmful addictions, and then pray for sudden healing. Pray for strength and help earlier.

God's world is a good world, and the very fact that good effects come from good causes is eloquent testimony, but just as clear proof is that bad effects come from bad causes. If you could ignore all the rules and come out unscarred, that would make it a bad world, not a good one. You may never have thought about it this way, but one of the strongest biblical affirmations that this is a good, or benevolent, world is the well-known warning, "Be not deceived; God is not mocked; for whatsoever a man soweth, that shall he also reap" (Gal. 6:7).

One of the main characters in *For Whom the Bell Tolls* says, "The world is a fine place and worth the fighting for and I hate very much to leave it." Try changing the quote slightly for yourself, saying, "The world is a fine place and worth the praying for and I hate very much to waste it."

In his great classic work on *The Will of God*, Leslie Weatherhead insisted that this is a good world and that the evil which happens in it is not the will of God. He says that calamity and distress are not in the intentional will of God, but "when you see his glory reflected in this lovely earth, in nature around us so full of his beauty, in poem and song, in picture, in music, in great architecture and in lowly service, in the lives of lovely people, in the happiness of a home, in the health of the body and the resilience of the mind and the saintliness of the soul, then, looking up to your Father in heaven, say, 'Thy will be done'; and let us so dedicate ourselves *that we may be made one in the glorious harmony of all things and all people who carry out his will*, that it may be done in earth as the angels do it in heaven."

CHAPTER TWELVE
A REDEMPTIVE WORLD

"Must I be carried to the skies
On flow'ry beds of ease,
While others fought to win the prize,
And sailed thro' bloody seas?

Are there no foes for me to face?
Must I not stem the flood?
Is this vile world a friend to grace,
To help me on to God?"

ISAAC WATTS, *Am I a Soldier of the Cross*

The above words express one of the most profound insights I have ever encountered about the Christian's attitude toward this imperfect world. The words which are especially provocative to me ask the probing question, "Is this vile world a friend to grace, to help me on to God?"

Perhaps you thought of the world as an alien place and an enemy force trying to keep you away from God. Watts suggests that you think of this world, with its foes and bloody seas, as a necessary part of God's redemptive plan.

Ask yourself: Is God using the lessons of my adversities to get me closer to him? Can my heartaches and hardships be turned into blessings instead of curses? Can my suffering become a source of strength for someone else?

Must the route to Easter morning go through the hill of Calvary?

If you answer yes to all the questions in the above paragraph, then you already understand what Isaac Watts was talking about. You have already developed a philosophy about adversity which is reflected in so many great thinkers, such as Shakespeare:

> *Sweet are the uses of adversity,*
> *Which, like the toad, ugly and venomous,*
> *Wears yet a precious jewel in his head;*
> *And this our life, exempt from public haunt,*
> *Finds tongues in trees, books in the*
>   *running brooks,*
> *Sermons in stones, and good in everything.*

During the time of Christ, the Greek philosopher Lucius Seneca observed that "Fire is the test of gold; adversity, of strong men." Centuries later Francis Bacon alluded to Seneca's observations with his own: "It was a high speech of Seneca that the good things which belong to prosperity are to be wished, but the good things that belong to adversity are to be admired."

Bacon also said that, "Prosperity doth best discover vice, but adversity doth best discover virtue."

Anne Bradstreet pointed out the necessity of adversity for appreciating our blessings: "If we had no winter, spring would not be so pleasant: if we did not sometimes taste of adversity, prosperity would not be so welcome."

Washington Irving painted a lovely picture of women's response to adversity: "There is in every true woman's heart a spark of heavenly fire, which lies dormant in the broad daylight of prosperity; but which kindles up, and beams and blazes in the dark horn of adversity."

All of these wise sages are recognizing the redemptive quality of the adversities of this hard world. They are implying that hardship is the real making of a person. They do not deny that the world is often cruel and unfair, but they affirm with Isaac Watts that "this vile world is a friend to grace to help us on to God."

Take another look at Paul's reaction to his thorn in the flesh: "Three times I begged the Lord about this to make it go away and leave me, but he said to me, 'My spiritual strength is sufficient, for it is only by means of conscious weakness that perfect power is developed.' So I most happily boast about my weaknesses, so that the strength of Christ may overshadow me. That is why I take such pleasure in weaknesses, insults, distresses, persecution, and difficulties which I endure for Christ's sake, for it is when I am consciously weak that I am really strong" (2 Cor. 12:8-10, WMS).

Paul did not have a pie-in-the-sky religion. He really knew how mean this world can be. But he said that that was what made him the man he was. In a very real way, the evil world became redemptive for him. It made him into a tower of strength. Of course, it was God's grace that did it, but the instrument in God's hand was a hostile world.

Jesus said, "And ye shall be hated of all men for my name's sake: but he that endureth to the end shall be saved" (Matt. 10:22).

The writer of Hebrews said, "If ye endure chastening, God dealeth with you as with sons" (Heb. 12:7).

James said, "Blessed is the man that endureth temptation: for when he is tried, he shall receive the crown of life, which the Lord hath promised to them that love him" (James 1:12).

All of these underscore the fact that God's blessings and rewards come to those who have responded to this world in a redemptive way, rather than in a defeatist way. They have said we will let this world make us better men, not bitter men.

In the final count, it is not what happens *to* you, but what happens *in* you that is most important. Your reaction to the world's buffeting reflects your relationship with God. The high priestly prayer of our Lord on behalf of his followers included a special prayer for us: "I do not pray that thou shouldest take them out of the world, but that thou shouldest keep them from the evil" (John 17:15).

Jesus does not want to deliver us from this world of

injustice and unrighteousness. He wants us to find in this very world our strength and maturity as children of God. This world is the arena where we are becoming what God wants us to be, the workshop where he is fashioning us for service above.

This means that our praying, which is to be in harmony with God's purpose, should be like the prayer of Jesus. We should not pray for deliverance from an unfriendly world, but for God's prevailing grace through our pilgrimage here.

Rather than trying to pinpoint causes and effects, we ought to be praying for wisdom to act in light of events. "As he was walking along, he saw a man blind from birth. 'Master,' his disciples asked him, 'why was this man born blind? Was it a result of his own sins or those of his parents?' 'Neither,' Jesus answered. 'But to demonstrate the power of God' " (John 9:1-3, TLB).

Jesus did two very significant things in the encounter with the blind man. He rejected the notion that all suffering is punishment for sin, and he became actively involved in relieving the man's misery. We need to follow Jesus' example in this story.

Too much of our praying is wasted in asking God, why? Too much effort and study is expended on the nature of problems rather than on the possible solutions.

Suppose a tornado or flood comes through your town, causing devastating damage, loss of life, and leaving many homeless. There are several different kinds of ways you can choose to react to the disaster:

1. You can question or even curse God for allowing, or causing, it to happen.
2. You can join philosophical discussions on the nature and meaning of such events.
3. You can move away or withdraw from the ugly scene.
4. You can accuse the victims of being great sinners to have brought such catastrophe upon themselves.
5. You can try to sort out in your theology as to whether this was the original will or permissive will of God.
6. You can pray for the victims and their families, make yourself and resources available to those in need. You can

also pray for personal strength to be equal to the need of the hour, and demonstrate such an overall compassionate spirit of unselfish service that the name of Christ will be honored and people will be brought closer to God by this experience because of your response to their need.

Surely, you can readily see which of these reactions is in harmony with God's will in making even a dangerous world a redemptive world.

Paul gives clear instruction for this kind of response: "So you must be very careful how you live, not thoughtlessly but thoughtfully, and continue to make the most of your opportunities, for the times are evil. So stop being senseless, but understand what the Lord's will is" (Eph. 5:15-17, WMS).

Go back over that last sentence and underline a very important word, *is:* "Understand what the Lord's will *is!*" Present tense, not past tense. He doesn't say, "Try to figure out what the will of the Lord *was*," but thoughtfully and sensibly, "understand what the Lord's will *is*."

When a disaster happens in your community the most productive kind of praying you can do is to ask what God's will *is* for you in the light of the present need. When reverses, or even tragedies, happen in your personal life, the best thing you can do for your welfare and growth is to ask God what he wants you to do *now*, in the present tense.

I am not saying that we should never try to understand God's will in retrospect. It is in seeing God's footprints in the past that we know how to recognize his presence and know where he is leading. But prayer cannot change the past. Prayer appropriates the present and shapes the future. Praying to know God's will and work in the present tense is the most direct way to make this a redemptive world.

One of my friends in college later came to be our minister of education. He and his wife were examples of faith and courage to us all. While on the way to the hospital to have their first child they were involved in a terrible car accident on the freeway, and Sue was thrown through the windshield of the car. Her severe injuries and radical treatment resulted in irreparable brain damage to their child. He lay flat on his back for over thirty years with the mind of an infant. To compound the tragedy he was struck with polio at an early age which brought more suffering and anxiety.

Without blaming God or becoming bitter, Sue and Glenn courageously and lovingly cared for Bobby in their own home all those years. Sue's constant prayer was that God would give her strength to care for him. That prayer was answered in abundance. Through all those years she was practically never ill and she developed an uncanny physical stamina in being able to lift and care for the grown body of her child.

They had two other children, and their home was a place of laughter and love. Their quiet testimony of faith and courage influenced all whose lives they touched. Their example of unselfishness caused many of us to reassess our own priorities. This is one of the finest examples I personally know where, through prayer and faith, a tragedy became a redemptive means of strengthening the character of many.

Of course, they would have chosen instead to have had a normal, healthy child, and all the good that came from their tragedy can never replace what they lost. But, the point is that the tragedy did happen, and they responded redemptively.

You cannot make everything come out right in your world. Suffering is inevitable: "Yet man is born unto trouble, as the sparks fly upward" (Job 5:7). The decisive factor is how you respond to that suffering.

Suffering and tragedy do not always result in building character and bringing man to God. When Jesus died on the cross two thieves hung on the crosses on either side of him. One of them cursed God and taunted Christ. The other recognized his own sinfulness and Christ's sinlessness and asked the Lord to remember him. In this simple, basic prayer, the dying thief allowed a cruel humiliating execution to bring him to faith in Christ and a promise of paradise.

Not only should we pray for God to make our own suffering a redemptive experience, but we should also pray that the suffering of others will make us more aware of desperate humanity and how we can help. In his book *In Search of Myself*, D. R. Davies told of visiting Spain in 1937 and observing the wretchedness of the poor. He wrote, "I passed through an experience in which I felt the magnitude of human frustration, pain and defeat. For a moment I gathered up in myself the suffering of hungry, baffled men and women. It went a long way to push me to my final despair." But it was also an important factor in bringing him to God. He continued, "In my bedroom before getting into bed I knelt down for the first time for years and cried, 'Oh, God!' That was all, but though I knew not God, that was, I believe, the deepest prayer I have ever uttered."

Elton Trueblood pointed out that there is a close connection between suffering and love. He said, "Suffering can be especially effective in bringing to men and women a sense of being loved." He also observed that life with no element of tragedy is almost sure to be superficial and self-centered.

Then, Dr. Trueblood made a striking connection between nature itself and humanity's experience of tragedy: "Ours is a universe of turmoil, and even our solar system, it is widely believed by experts, began with a major disturbance. Starting in the tumult of great tides, the history of our own small planet has itself been tumultuous. There has been the fierceness of cold and heat, the harsh struggle for survival, the rise and fall of species. But it all seems to be pointing somewhere, in the direction of more life, more mind, more spirit in the sense of the self-conscious appreciation of what ought to be. Could it have come without the tumult, the pain, and the endless struggle?"

This brings us back to Isaac Watts' question in his immortal hymn: "Is this vile world a friend to grace, to help me on to God?" The answer of the growing Christian must be a victorious "Yes!" And his prayers must be triumphant prayers that seek to work in harmony with nature in order that even a cruel world may become a redemptive world.

At the close of this main section on praying in harmony with nature, another symbol of harmonious prayer is added. Recalling that the uniform circles represent our PSM in harmony with each other, now is added the third band of nature which flows in harmony with the bands representing God and self.

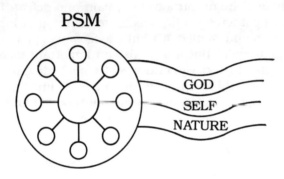

PART

5

Answers in Harmony with Christ's Words

"He chose to include the things
That in each other are included,
The whole, the complicate,
The amassing harmony."
WALLACE STEVENS
It Must Give Pleasure

ANSWERS to prayers come in many shapes, sizes, and names. Even the idea of what constitutes a prayer answer varies greatly among believers. The next time you are in a small group discussing prayer, ask those in the group to tell how they think God answers prayer. The most outstanding thing about their response will be the variety of answers. The participants will be surprised themselves to learn that everyone doesn't think alike about answered prayer.

This should not be confusing or discouraging to you. Instead, it should reinforce your faith in a heavenly Father who can answer all of his many children in the great variety of ways needed. This means he can answer so that you, too, can be sure of his presence and power in your life.

Some people insist that every prayer must be answered literally as it is asked, or there has been no answer. Some say that God answers generally the prayers of mankind and that we are to fill in the specific blanks. Others insist that the whole idea is for us to get in the right frame of mind so that we can solve our own problems.

Some agree with George Meredith, who said, "Who rises from prayer a better man, his prayer is answered." Others feel that this gives prayer only a psychological effect, rather than real power.

It has been said so often that some people probably think it's a biblical teaching that God always answers: sometimes yes, sometimes no, and sometimes wait.

How does God answer prayer? The response is almost endless: through opportunities, through Scripture, through direct inspiration, in dreams, by closed doors, by sermon, song, and worship, through wisdom gained by experience, in the wise counsel of friends, by physical intervention, in spiritual illumination, in intellectual knowledge, by speaking, by remaining silent, by promoting you, by restraining you, etc., etc., etc.

Are any of these answers right? They can all be right. You must allow God to answer as God chooses to answer. You must never insist that he answer you as he did someone else, or the way in which you decide is best.

There is one criterion for a valid prayer answer: it must be in harmony with the words of Jesus Christ. Paul wrote, "Though we, or an angel from heaven, preach any other gospel unto you than that which we have preached unto you, let him be accursed" (Gal. 1:8). The same principle applies to a prayer answer. It doesn't make any difference if it comes from a famous preacher, or a vision, or a voice, or an angel from heaven, if it does not correspond to the teachings of Jesus Christ, it is not from God.

One of Jesus' most famous prayer promises was: "I say unto you, ask, and it shall be given you; seek, and ye shall find; knock, and it shall be opened unto you. For everyone who asks receives, and he who seeks finds, and to him who knocks it will be opened" (Luke 11:9, 10).

I am not suggesting that Jesus was giving any secret clues to answered prayer. I believe this was his poetic and comprehensive way of speaking. But, I would like to suggest that three types of prayers and answers can be paralleled with these words of Jesus, and can serve as a pattern for knowing and responding to God's prayer answers.

The first is "ask and receive," the second is "seek and find," and the third is "knock and open." These will form the basis for these last three chapters on answers that are in harmony with Christ's words. We will call these received answers, found answers, and opened answers.

We began our search by noting that our prayers must be in harmony with each other. We end our search by discovering that the answers to our prayers must be in harmony with Christ's words. In between these two we have seen that we must pray in harmony with God, self, and nature.

In the little symbol of prayer which we have been building, the circles in harmony with each other represent our PSM (Primary, Secondary, and Motive prayer). Flowing out of those circles are the bands which represent praying in harmony with God, self, and nature.

Now, add another circle to the right side of the symbol, which will represent the answers to our prayers. Above this circle write the initials RFO which stand for Receive, Find, and Open, the key words in the promise from Luke 11:10. As we progress through these last chapters we will see how our PSM and our RFO are brought together by praying in harmony with God, self, and nature.

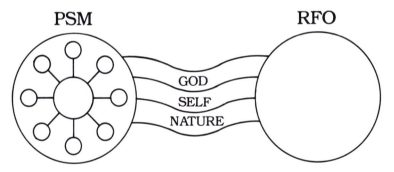

CHAPTER THIRTEEN
EVERYONE WHO ASKS RECEIVES

"God answers sharp and sudden on
  some prayers,
And thrusts the thing we have prayed for
  in our face,
A gauntlet with a gift in 't."

ELIZABETH BARRETT BROWNING, *Aurora Leigh*

It is true that everything we have comes from God: "Every good gift and every perfect gift is from above, and cometh down from the Father of lights" (James 1:17). But, the Bible's teachings on prayer seem to indicate that there are special blessings beyond our common provisions which are available to those who ask for them.

Another passage from James is: "You do not have, because you do not ask. You ask and do not receive, because you ask wrongly, to spend it on your passions" (James 4:2, 3, RSV). The last half of this passage was dealt with in our chapter on motive prayer. But we ought to look closely at the first half: "You do not have because you do not ask."

A frequent question about prayer is, "Why do I need to pray if God already knows what I need and want?" This is a logical question, because Jesus did indeed say, "Your Father knoweth what things ye have need of, before ye ask him" (Matt. 6:8).

Many have attempted to answer the question. Some books on prayer devote a great deal of space to the probable reasons why an omniscient (all knowing) God requires his people to ask for his blessings. These are usually very helpful insights and interesting speculations. But, the truth is none of us really knows the answer. We humans try to compare our experiences with God's nature, and of course there can be no satisfactory comparison.

We do not know why God tells us to pray for what he already knows we need. But we do know that he tells us to. The dedicated disciple obeys because the Master has spoken, not because he understands or agrees with the Master. Stonewall Jackson once said, "My duty is to obey orders." So it should be with the soldiers of the cross.

Mark records two incidents of Jesus requiring men to articulate their requests. James and John asked him if he would grant a special favor to them. "And he said to them, 'What do you want me to do for you?'" (Mark 10:36, RSV). Later he encountered blind Bartimaeus in Jericho, and when the blind man rose and ran to Jesus, the Lord asked him, "What do you want me to do for you?" (10:51, RSV).

Jesus knew the desires of these men, but he wanted them to tell him. This sort of encounter happened many times during Jesus' ministry. He was always trying to get people to communicate with him, to tell their deepest longings. It seemed as though he was holding something special for those who would ask. These thoughts remind me of the famous lines from James Russell Lowell:

> *For a cap and bells our lives we pay,*
> *Bubbles we buy with the whole soul's tasking:*
> *'Tis heaven alone is given away,*
> *'Tis only God may be had for the asking.*

Asking and receiving go hand in hand just as do seeking and finding (which we will look at in the next chapter). Achieving is one thing, but receiving is quite another. Achieving is something I can do. Receiving means accepting what someone else has done. Both achieving and receiving have their legitimate place in the Christian life. It will help clear up a lot of questions when you learn to keep the distinction between achieving and receiving.

For instance, salvation is by receiving the grace of God, not by the achievement of good works (Eph. 2:8, 9). But fulfilling God's intention for our lives is achieved by the doing of his will (Eph. 2:10). We achieve growth and maturity here on earth, but we receive eternal life as his gift (Rom. 6:23).

We achieve many good things in this life because we have worked for them and earned them, and that is as it should be. In fact, I am one who doubts that we ought to ask God for anything we can honorably achieve for ourselves.

There are, however, many things which we can receive only through direct answer to prayer. Receiving straight from God things we cannot achieve for ourselves is a very distinct kind of answer which harmonizes with the teachings of Christ.

Immediately following his exhortation about asking, seeking, and knocking, Jesus said, "Your heavenly Father [will] give the Holy Spirit to them that ask him" (Luke 11:13). This is something you cannot achieve for yourself. The indwelling Christ comes to those who ask him to come in.

I have already mentioned receiving salvation, but Paul specifically related it to prayer: "For whosoever shall call upon the name of the Lord shall be saved."

Knowledge is something you can achieve through study and observation, but spiritual wisdom or discernment can be received only from God. "If any of you lacks wisdom, let him ask God, who gives to all men generously and without reproaching, and it will be given him" (James 1:5, RSV).

The supporting presence of God in trouble is something you cannot work up; you receive it with a trusting heart: "He shall call upon me, and I will answer him; I will be with him in trouble; I will deliver him, and honour him" (Ps. 91:15). "Thou shalt call . . . and he shall say, Here I am" (Isa. 58:9).

Receiving a special enduement to turn tragedy into triumph (such as we discussed in the chapter on a redemptive world) is definitely a grace gift from God: "And I will bring the third part through the fire, and will refine them as silver is refined, and will try them as gold is tried; they shall call on my name, and I will hear them" (Zech. 13:9).

6) Forgiveness of sins cannot be achieved by doing pennance or merits of righteousness, but only by receiving his gracious response to our prayer of confession: "If we confess our sins, he is faithful and just to forgive us our sins, and to cleanse us from all unrighteousness" (1 John 1:9).

The key to understanding how our prayer is being answered is to try to understand the difference between achieving and receiving. This is clear in the scriptural examples just given, even though it is not always easy to follow through on them. But, there are many times when there is uncertainty about *achieving* and *receiving*, whether we should do something ourselves, or wait for God to do it. How much of the answer is the product of our working or our waiting? For example, in looking for a job, how much is achieving and how much is receiving? In meeting your obligations, is that your responsibility in work, or God's responsibility in providence?

In the Sermon on the Mount, Jesus spoke about our creaturely needs such as clothing and food, and reminded us that our "heavenly Father knoweth that ye have need of all these things" (Matt. 6:32). Then he instructed us to "seek ye first the kingdom of God, and his righteousness; and all these things shall be added unto you" (6:33).

After we have done all that we can and should in our responsibility as children of God, we can trust the heavenly Father to provide our necessities. But, there are special things which we pray for because no one but God can do anything for us. Asking and receiving become a very conscious reality to us.

In one of our earliest pastorates, the church embarked upon a building program, and my wife and I prayed and felt led to pledge a certain amount to the building fund. We thought we had it figured out so we could do it, but unforeseen emergencies cleaned us out, and we did not see any way to pay our pledge when it was due. We felt very strongly that our influence and example was even more important than the actual amount of money involved. So, we told God that the only way we could keep our commitment was for his direct intervention. The next day when my wife went downtown, she stepped out of the car and stepped on a coin purse which had obviously been dropped earlier. The purse contained to the penny exactly the amount of our pledge (I've never understood why it would have hurt to have included a little extra spending money). We took the money to the police station, advertised over the radio and in the paper, and after no one came forward to claim it, we paid our pledge to the church.

This was obviously a *receiving* answer. I had done all I could do and still could not meet my obligations. I took the matter to the Lord and left it there. I did not try to tell him how to do it. I did absolutely nothing to earn or deserve that bonus. It was a gift received, and a commitment honored.

Timing is often a helpful measure in assessing a received answer. God is not bound by time, and works as it pleases his purpose. One of the most cherished prayer promises in the Bible is Isaiah 65:24, "And it shall come to pass that before they call, I will answer; and while they are yet speaking, I will hear." How thrilling to know that God is working in your behalf even before you pray. He knows what you are going to pray and has the answer on the way.

Nearly all of us have had experiences of praying for specific news or needs, and receiving the answer in the mail that very day or the next day. The answer could not possibly have reached us then unless it had been mailed before we prayed. When this happens we stand in awe of a great and caring God at work behind the scenes, and all we can do is *receive* his answer.

Another good measure of a received answer is the element of secrecy. All prayer does not have to be in secret. We are admonished to pray together and to share our prayer concerns with the church. But, there are some special times when we ought to pray alone. For those times, Jesus told us, "Enter into thy closet, and when thou hast shut the door, pray to thy Father which is in secret; and thy Father which seeth in secret shall reward thee openly" (Matt. 6:6).

When you have told no one else, have not hinted to anyone about your need, and it comes exactly as you prayed in secret, it is a holy moment for you as you stand humbly receiving the answer.

After I passed my qualifying exams to continue my doctoral studies I was told that I was weak in three areas and the committee was requiring that I take nine more hours of remedial courses. I was extremely frustrated by this turn of events. I had completed (I thought) all my campus course work and had only the dissertation to write. I had moved to a new pastorate about 200 miles from the university. It was a large church, involved in expansion plans, and I could see no way of going back to the campus for those three courses.

My wife and I talked and prayed about the dilemma, but told no one else. I didn't even ask any of the church leaders if they thought we could work it out. I made no contact with any of the university faculty or administration, but I took the matter in secret prayer to the Lord. I told him that I had felt his leadership every step of the way in getting this degree, and now it looked like I had reached an insurmountable obstacle unless he intervened.

After several weeks of silence, I decided that some move had to be made. So, I drove back to Baylor University in Waco and went in to talk to the chairman of the department. I had rehearsed my speech to tell him that I felt my first obligation was to my new pastorate, that I could not do those extra courses, and that I would have to either drop out of the program or get an extension of time.

Before I could even begin my speech, Dr. Summers said, "Bill, I'm glad you came in today. I've been wanting to talk to you. We have been reviewing your work again, and we don't see any need for you to do those remedial courses. So, just try to get started on your dissertation when you can."

I will never forget how I felt then and a few minutes later as I stood outside on that beautiful spring day. I was overwhelmed with the awesome power and tender concern of the heavenly Father. Without my saying a word to a soul who could possibly have influenced such a decision, God had quietly done his work.

About an hour after I finished writing the above paragraphs about praying in secret, I received a telephone call that left me weak in the knees but strong in the heart.

I had been giving myself completely to finishing the writing of this book, and had not taken any speaking engagements. Consequently, the financial situation had become extremely critical. Also, about a month before my wife and I were both struck down by a van while crossing the street. We were in and out of hospitals and doctor's offices for several weeks. So, things had not been ideal while I was trying to write a book about prayer and faith.

Just that morning we were going over our bills, and I told Margie that we would have to borrow a thousand dollars to pay the monthly bills, and I frankly didn't know where to go for it. We had both been praying earnestly about our finances, but secretly between us and God. We had exhausted every effort we knew.

As I wrote that part about praying in secret, I was in the very process of doing what I was writing about. I was imploring God to do something about the predicament which seemed to be beyond our control. Then, within the hour I received a telephone call from a friend who said a relative of his in another town where I had preached months ago had sent a check to me for exactly one thousand dollars, the very amount we needed that very week. It seems uncanny that it happened at exactly the time I was writing the chapter about praying in secret, and receiving God's gift answers.

Sometimes asking and receiving are so closely connected that the answer seems to be a part of the prayer, or to put it another way, the prayer answers itself. You may be praying for God to convict someone that they should teach a class, or witness to a certain person who is lost. In your concern and intense praying, you become convicted yourself and volunteer to teach, or go and witness. In effect, you have become an answer to your own prayer. Of course, I think you should always pray with that possibility open. Don't ask God to make other people do something you are not willing to do yourself.

Sometimes as soon as you have voiced the prayer, the answer appears in your mind. The solution becomes clear once the problem has been stated. These are obvious received answers which God's Spirit communicates to your spirit. But you must be willing to receive.

After several months of continuous Bible conferences, my wife and I were really missing the fellowship and opportunities for personal service which only a pastorate can give. Driving home after a week's engagement, we were nearing our city about midnight and we were sharing our mutual prayer concern that God would give us pastoral ministry opportunities in addition to preaching assignments.

We were so engrossed in talking about how much we missed ministering to people in need that we almost didn't see the stalled car beside the road. A young mother with three small children was driving from South Texas to Chicago with barely enough money to buy gas. A tire had blown out and she had run down her battery sitting with her lights on waiting for someone to stop. After we got her car going again, we took her and the children to our home to spend the night and get some home cooking. I got a local tire dealer to give her a couple of new tires the next day and we sent her on with a little extra money to help. We got a beautiful letter of appreciation about a week later. She told us she had been sitting there praying and praying for God to send somebody to her and her children. We had been praying for opportunities to help. In his infinite wisdom God had synchronized those prayers in perfect harmony.

Don't be surprised some day if in the middle of your prayer, God interrupts and says, "I'm glad you mentioned that. I've been wanting to ask you to do that yourself." You could be an answer to your own prayer, an answer which God gives and you receive in humility and surrender.

At this point we make another addition to our symbol, within the RFO circle. It is an arrow coming straight from heaven to you. This is an answer you simply receive because you have asked.

RFO

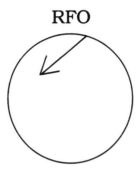

CHAPTER FOURTEEN
HE WHO SEEKS FINDS

"Nothing is so difficult but that it may be found out by seeking."

TERENCE

"Seek ye first the kingdom of God,
and his righteousness, and all
these things shall be added unto
you" (Matthew 6:33).

There are basically two ways of getting what we need and want in life: by reception and by action, or by *receiving* and *seeking*. In the last chapter we discussed the first way, that of reception, simply receiving what is given. This chapter examines the prayer which begins with seeking.

Too many people stop at Jesus' first word on prayer, "Ask and ye shall receive." That is all they hear and all they really want to hear. To them, praying is their part and giving is God's part. They sit, waiting for God to supply their needs. There are, indeed, many prayer answers that are *received answers,* but there is also a legitimate place in your prayer life for *found answers.*

Jesus said, "Seek and you will find . . . he who seeks finds," in the specific context of teaching about prayer. His disciples said, "Lord, teach us to pray" (Luke 11:1). In response, Jesus taught them the Lord's Prayer (vv. 2-4). Following that he told the story of the friend who came at midnight, illustrating persistency in prayer (vv. 5-8). In the following verses we read about the heavenly Father who gives good gifts to his children who pray. In the midst of all this comes the "ask, seek, and knock" passage (vv. 8-10).

So, the admonition to "seek and find" is not related here to intellectual pursuits or treasure hunts. It is an integrated part of the prayer process. Getting what you pray for often depends on your seeking and finding, just as it sometimes means asking and receiving.

The Bible repeatedly instructs us to seek God, who is the source and ground of all that we pray for. As Moses was preparing the people to enter the promised land of Canaan, he said, "If from thence thou shalt seek the Lord thy God, thou shalt find him, if thou seek him with all thy heart and with all thy soul" (Deut. 4:29).

Centuries later, settled in the conquered land, the descendants of Moses' followers heard their shepherd-king David repeat the same exhortation, "Seek the Lord, and his strength: seek his face evermore" (Ps. 105:4).

Then came the clarion call of the prophet Isaiah, "Seek ye the Lord while he may be found, call ye upon him while he is near (Isa. 55:6). The compassionate Hosea added his plea, "It is time to seek the Lord, till he come and rain righteousness upon you" (Hos. 10:12).

When the apostle Paul stood in Athens to address the learned philosophers, he implored "that they should seek God, in the hope that they might feel after him and find him. Yet he is not far from each one of us" (Acts 17:27, RSV).

Thus, when Jesus of Nazareth told his disciples that seeking and finding is an integral part of praying, he was in the mainstream of biblical teaching on spiritual discovery.

All of this emphasis on seeking and finding is to say that there are some prayer answers which you must find yourself. This does not make it any less an activity of prayer. You should still take the need to God. You still use all the guidelines suggested in our previous chapters. You still trust God to answer, but you allow him to answer as he chooses. And sometimes he chooses to answer by leading you to search and discover.

The first place to search for prayer answers is in the Bible itself. When the Word of God gives clear instructions, you already have your answer. You do not need to wait for further inspiration or instruction. You need only to act on the answer that is there.

A young couple once told me that they did not know what God wanted them to do about tithing. They said they were still praying about it and that he had not answered them yet. I pointed out that he had, indeed, answered them. God's word about tithing is already abundantly and permanently recorded. All the praying in the world will not change what the Bible says about your responsibility in stewardship. Search the Scriptures, for there is your answer.

Two men in one of our churches were bitter enemies and had the church divided over their enmity. One of them was ready to reconcile, but the other said he was still praying about it. I told him he was wasting his time praying, that the Bible already contained the answer. When he responded privately, and then publicly, to scriptural instructions about reconciliation with Christian brothers, our church experienced a beautiful revival.

I have witnessed to people who have said they don't know what to do about making a public profession of faith and joining a church, and they were honestly praying about it. I have led them to search the Scriptures for their answer, and have insisted that God is not going to tell them something different than he has told all believers what to do about his Son and his church.

Recently a young couple came to see me about their relationship. They were living together, although not married. They said they were both Christian and wanted to do God's will, and were praying about it, but he had not given them an answer. I said, "Oh, but he has. His answer is very clearly spelled out in the Scriptures. He will not give you a special message which contradicts his Word. Search the Scriptures, and do what he says there."

If you have not *received* the answer to a prayer you have been praying a good while, God may be wanting you to *find* the answer. The first place to start is in the Bible. The very answer you may have been waiting for may be waiting for you in the pages of God's Word.

A lot of times we interpret Jesus' words "seek and find" to mean that we should keep looking until we get what we want. What he means, instead, is that we should seek until we find what God has prepared for us. The *found* answer is the finding of God's will and God's provision.

This brings up the fascinating subject of serendipity. Some of your most exciting found answers will be in the form of a serendipity experience. Sir Horace Walpole first coined the word "serendipity" in 1754, basing it on a Persian fairy tale, *Three Princes of Serendip*. Serendip was the ancient or Arabic name for the island now called Sri Lanka. The legend was that every time the princes of Serendip went on a journey something unexpected happened; by coincidence they found valuable things which they were not seeking. Sir Horace called this experience of finding things not sought (while often in quest of something else) by the intriguing word "serendipity."

Many of the great discoveries and advancements of civilization have been serendipity experiences. Emerson said, "Columbus was looking for a direct route to Asia, and stubbed his toe on America." Edison was looking for the electric light when he found the phonograph. Louis Pasteur was looking for a way to keep wine from turning sour, and found the process of pasteurization.

William Roentgen, a professor in a Bavarian university, was working with the vacuum tube for improved photography when he saw some unusual fluorescent action that led him to develop X-ray. Alexander Fleming was working in the laboratory at the Hospital of St. Mary when dust from an open window contaminated some plate cultures, which led Fleming to the discovery of penicillin.

Alexander Graham Bell was trying to improve the telegraph when he developed the telephone. Charles Goodyear was trying to get the stickiness out of rubber when he developed vulcanizing. Dr. William Pollard says that no one was deliberately looking for an atomic bomb, which evolved from the combined work of many different scientists.

Jesus told a serendipity story about a man who was plowing a field and came across buried treasure. He said the kingdom of God is like that. Many treasures get added unexpectedly in the Christian pursuit of life. "Seek ye first the kingdom of God, . . . and all these things shall be added unto you" (Matt. 6:33).

If you feel led to seek the answer to your prayer, don't be too surprised if God gives you some additional answers along the way. His leading you out to seek may be his way of exposing you to other needs you didn't even know you had.

> He was a Christian and he prayed.
> He asked for strength to do greater things;
> He was given infirmity that he might do better things.
> He asked for riches that he might be happy;
> He was given poverty that he might be wise.
> He asked for power to have the praise of men;
> He was given weakness to feel the need of God.
> He received nothing that he asked for;
> But all that he hoped for.
> His prayer seems unanswered,
> But he is most blessed.

One of your biggest surprises may be that you will discover your answer in your own backyard. In his famous lecture "Acres of Diamonds," Russell Conwell told the story of an ancient Persian named Al Hafed, who owned a large farm. One day a Buddhist priest told Al Hafed of the rich splendor of diamonds to be found in some parts of the world. Discontented, Al Hafed sold his farm and set out to search throughout the world for his fortune in diamonds. It was a fruitless search which left him discouraged and penniless, and he drowned himself in the sea. In the meantime, the person who had bought Al Hafed's farm discovered literally acres of diamonds on the land of the man who had plodded wearily over the earth seeking riches.

Don't overlook the answers that may be the easiest to find and the closest to home. We will look at the possibilities suggested here more in depth in our last chapter.

In your search for God's answer to your prayer, don't settle for second best. This isn't the same as serendipity. In the serendipity experience you receive an additional blessing you were not expecting, and it is often better than what you had sought. But, sometimes we lower our standards and are willing to settle for just something, lest we end up with nothing. One reason we are often dissatisfied with our praying is because we lose patience waiting for God, start looking for the answer, and accept the first reasonable facsimile.

Sometimes we simply do not aim high enough to begin with. You have to think big and stretch tall to do business with God. Emerson said, "Hitch your wagon to a star," and the apostle Paul said it like this: "Set your affection on things above, not on things on the earth" (Col. 3:2).

The penalty for misplaced affections is that we end up with ceilings that are too low for a man to stand up under. You may think that you would be satisfied if God would answer your prayers for success and prosperity, but as high as they seem, these can also be ceilings that are too low.

> *For those who seek the answer in*
> *Houses, lands, and rings,*
> *Will some day find that empty lives*
> *Are just as empty filled with things.*

Pray that God will enable you to climb great heights of spiritual maturity and humility. Then, seek the answer to that prayer by studying the lives of spiritual giants to discover their secret.

Pray that God will give you the opportunity to perform an unusually high and noble service. Find the answer to that prayer by looking in your immediate neighborhood for someone in desperate need of assistance.

Pray that God will make you a special kind of loving person. Discover the answer to that prayer by going out of your way to befriend an especially unlovable person.

Pray that God will give you one of the most important jobs in the world. Seek and find the answer to that dream in teaching a small child.

Pray that you will be an outstanding leader of men. Find your answer to that courageous prayer in diligent study, preparation, integrity, and loyalty.

Pray that you will get and keep all that is rightfully yours. Then, go and discover the answer by giving yourself away to others.

Pray that you will be able to understand and emulate the spirit of Christ. Find your answer in forgiving those who have persecuted you and crucified you.

Do you dare to pray as high as I am suggesting? It is nothing to ask God for money and position and health. Do you dare ask him to take you into the highest of high and holy of holies with Christ?

> *Thou art coming to a King,*
> *Large petitions with thee bring.*
> *For his grace and power are such*
> *None can ever ask too much.*

But in the kind of praying I have just suggested, the answers are *found,* not *received.* God will not give you forgiveness until you forgive. He will not make you a leader until you are true and loyal and ready. He will not make you great until you humble yourself. These are answers you must seek and find!

All of this implies an image of God which may be contrary to your usual picture of him when you pray. Perhaps you usually think of yourself as waiting in faith and patience for the "God who acts." This is good and appropriate for *received* answers, but for the *found* answers of your life you need to get acquainted with the "God who waits."

Wallace Hamilton wrote that God "is not the Almighty

Dictator, the Grand Sultan of the universe, pushing people around and snapping his fingers to get his will done in a hurry. He is the God who waits—with infinite patience he waits."

There is a double-edged sword in this word from Isaiah: "Therefore the Lord will wait, that he may be gracious to you; and therefore will he be exalted, that he may have mercy upon you: for the Lord is a God of judgment: blessed are all they that wait for him" (Isa. 30:18).

We are accustomed to being told that we should be like "those who wait for him," but Isaiah says in addition to our waiting for the Lord, that God is also waiting for us. Patiently, lovingly, God is waiting.

He waited a long time for men to grasp the idea of monotheism—faith in one God. He waited longer still for men to see their essential unity in brotherhood. He is still waiting for us to discover the way of peace.

Henry van Dyke's poem is about God, who patiently waits for man to discover what he had wanted for man all along:

> *One day God said, "I'm tired of kings!"*
> *But that was a long time ago,*
> *And man kept saying, "No:*
> *I like their looks in robes and rings . . ."*
> *So he crowned a few more,*
> *And the kings as before*
> *Kept fighting and spoiling things.*
> *But at last man said, "I'm tired of kings!*
> *Sons of the robber chiefs of yore,*
> *They make me pay for their lust and their war,*
> *I am the puppet: they pull the strings!*
> *The blood of my heart is the wine they drink,*
> *I shall govern myself for a while, I think,*
> *And see what that brings."*
> *Then God (who had made the first remark)*
> *Smiled in the dark.*

God is not absent. He is simply patient. You have been thinking of yourself as the patient one, waiting on God to

He Who Seeks Finds

answer your prayers. Now, see God as the patient One, waiting on you to see and find the answers he has waiting for you.

Seeking and finding may be a risky business for you. It is so much more secure to stay where you are. But, there are things of God we cannot have until we are ready to leave the security of what God has done for the insecurity of what he is doing and will do.

In *The Explorer*, Rudyard Kipling sends a thrill through our heart with the ringing challenge:

> *Something hidden. Go and find it. Go and*
>   *look behind the Ranges—*
> *Something lost behind the Ranges. Lost and*
>   *waiting for us. Go!*

Now, that we have seen that some of our answers may be *found* as well as *received*, another small symbol is added. The symbol for received answers is an arrow coming directly from God to you. The symbol for found answers is an arrow going out from you to search for God's waiting answer.

RFO

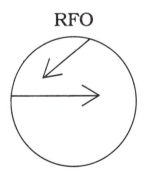

CHAPTER FIFTEEN
TO HIM WHO KNOCKS IT WILL BE OPENED

"Footfalls echo in the memory
Down the passage which we did not take
Towards the door we never opened."

THOMAS STEARNS ELIOT, *Four Quartets*

True answers to prayer must be in harmony with the words of Jesus Christ, as we discussed earlier. According to Luke 11:9-10, some are *received* answers, some are *found* answers, and some are *opened* answers. This last chapter discusses *opened* answers as a long overlooked possibility in getting what you pray for.

A door has two sides and can be opened from either. Thus, it is appropriate to think of knocking on a door from either side. The Bible speaks of this knocking on both sides. In Revelation 3:20, Jesus says, "Behold, I stand at the door and knock." But in our text for this chapter, Jesus tells us to "knock and it will be opened."

Where Jesus is knocking, waiting for us to open the door, we have *received* answers. Where we are standing and knocking (as in the Luke passage), we have *found* answers. But neither *received* answers nor *found* answers can be appropriated and utilized until they become *opened* answers.

Answers in Harmony with Christ's Words

Jesus made it clear that the blessing of his presence is conditional on our willingness to heed his knock: "If any man hear my voice, and open the door, I will come in to him, and will sup with him, and he with me" (Rev. 3:20). The responsibility of response is still ours, even though Jesus himself stands knocking.

Perhaps you have usually thought of prayer as a two-sided or double-action process, with you asking and God answering. There is a third action involved, and ignoring this third action keeps many people from realizing the answer to their prayers. This third action is simply opening the answer once you have received it.

If someone gives you a gift, you are eager to tear off the wrapping and open the box to see what treasure is there. Can you imagine just setting the gift down unopened and going your way? Or, can you see the folly of guessing at the contents, or comparing the size with another, or admiring the wrapping, while the real gift is waiting inside? That sounds foolish, but that is exactly what we do with some of God's answers to our prayers.

You may have been discouraged about your prayer life, and pretty well convinced that you are not very spiritual or don't have much faith because you have so many "unanswered" prayers on your record. That may honestly be the case, and you may need to review some, if not all, of the material in the previous chapters. There may be some unconfessed sin blocking your communication with God. There may be a total misunderstanding of how to pray in faith. You might really need to learn the meaning of praying in Jesus' name. I do not want to give you a false sense of assurance if you do have some spiritual problems that need correcting.

On the other hand, it is possible that you have the concept of prayer and the practice of prayer fairly well synchronized and you really feel that you have been praying in harmony with God, yourself, and nature. But, you still don't seem to be getting a very high percentage of your requests granted.

But you may be more successful in praying than you realize. God may be granting your prayer requests more readily and abundantly than you could believe. If that is so, why aren't you aware of it? The reason may be that you have not opened the answers God has given, or you have not walked through the door that was opened when you knocked.

How is this possible? Why would you pray and pray for something, and then not even open it when it comes? To understand how that happens to all of us who pray, notice the interesting story in the Book of Acts.

The persecution against the young church in Jerusalem had just begun. Herod had slain James and imprisoned Peter. The tiny band of believers huddled in prayer in the home of Mark's mother. "Peter therefore was kept in prison, but prayer was made without ceasing of the church unto God for him" (Acts 12:5).

That sounds like a God-honoring, Christ-centered, Bible-based prayer. It seemed to meet all the requirements for the kind of prayer God would answer. It was persistent prayer. It was offered to God (faith obviously in him, not themselves or methods). It was intercessory prayer, offered unselfishly for someone else. It was united prayer of the faith community, the church. That is the kind of prayer you would expect God to answer. And he did!

In a marvelous demonstration of his power, God sent an angel to Peter, who led him past the guards, and through the gate which swung open of its own accord. Once outside, the angel left Peter, who stood amazed at his miraculous deliverance. He then made his way quickly to the home where the church was gathered in prayer.

Peter knocked at the gate of the courtyard surrounding the house, and a maid named Rhoda was sent to see who was knocking. Peter called out to her, and she was so overcome with the joy of hearing his voice, that she ran back into the house to tell the others that Peter, the very one they were praying for, was standing outside.

They did not believe her, some even suggesting that she was beside herself. When she insisted that she was not mad, but that Peter was outside, they decided that it must be his ghost, or an angel. "But Peter continued knocking; and when they had opened the door and saw him, they

Answers in Harmony with Christ's Words

were astonished" (Acts 12:12). How many people are astonished when they get definite, literal answers to their prayers! They pray and pray *in faith*, and when the request is granted, they say, "I can't believe it!"

At an extremely critical time in one of our pastorates, one of our staff ministers left, and I called upon the church to pray with me that God would send us someone quickly, for the situation demanded an immediate replacement. Within a matter of days, the perfect person surfaced, one whom I had never in my life heard of before. Everything moved smoothly and quickly and he was on the field working in record time.

Some of the people were terribly agitated. They said that it was impossible to get someone that quickly unless it had already been schemed and prearranged. God had answered literally the exact prayer they had prayed (and I heard some of the complainers actually pray the prayer) for a speedy replacement, and they refused to accept the fact that God could do it.

The crucial part of the verse, however, is the first part: "Now Peter continued knocking." God had answered their prayer, above and beyond their highest expectations, but the literal answer, Peter himself, was standing outside knocking. They had a *received* answer, but they did not have an *opened* answer! God had given them what they asked, but they had not opened the door to let the answer in.

You may be more effective in praying than you think. God may have already given you the answer, but you have not opened the door to let it in. Why? There are many reasons why we keep God's answers outside our doors, but notice a few suggested by this story of Peter and the church.

The first obstacle to getting the answer past the gate was undisciplined emotion. Rhoda was so thrilled at the sound of Peter's voice, for joy she ran to tell the rest—leaving Peter standing outside, vulnerable to the posse that was probably hot on his trail. Dear sentimental Rhoda! You are not the first nor the last to be so caught up in emotional religion that you forget practical duties. It is understandable and commendable to be happy, Rhoda, but what you really need to do is to lift that latch and let Peter in.

There may be an undisciplined emotion which is keeping you from claiming God's answer by doing your duty. It can be a positive emotion of joy, sentiment, inspiration, aspiration, anticipation, love, or simply feeling good. It can be a negative emotion of doubt, fear, guilt, anger, hatred, or simply feeling bad. Any emotion which keeps you from doing what you should do is going to block God's answers from getting to you. If you are concentrating on an emotion, feeding it and giving way to it, that is a very good clue as to why you haven't been able to find many prayer answers lately.

Another obstacle to Peter's entrance was critical analysis. Though they were disciples who had walked with Jesus and were even now in united prayer, they could not take the simple answer to their prayer without questioning it.

First, they questioned Rhoda. They concluded that she must have mental problems, "Thou art mad." Isn't it strange how we always suppose that people who have had higher religious experiences than we have had are "just a little off?" We never question the mentality of those with less religion, just those with more. The truth is that we should be willing to let God reveal himself through a little maid or any humble servant he chooses. Don't question God's choice of instruments or voices by which he speaks to you.

The second analysis they performed was on the "thing" Rhoda insisted that she had seen. Well, if she is so insistent, maybe she did see something or hear something. If it resembled Peter, it must mean that he has already been executed and his ghost has returned, or maybe it was his guardian angel. Oh, the irony of it all! While God's full and gracious answer was standing knocking, his church leaders were having a theological debate. Sound familiar?

Rather than arguing about whether it is possible, or whether it may turn out to be just a ghost of what you prayed for (which is all that many of us expect), try simply believing that it is real. Don't be so theological and philosophical when you pray. Talk to God about real needs and hurts and expect him to answer with real solutions and comfort.

Yet another obstacle to getting the answer inside was their intellectual certainty. No, they were not highly educated people, but they were sure they knew how God would work. There was just no basis for expecting the kind of answer they got. They undoubtedly had already begun to speculate among themselves as to how God would answer; or they may have decided to *find* the answer with their own aggressive action. But they knew it could not happen the way Rhoda said it had.

Intellectual certainty is not the sole possession of those with advanced degrees. It happens at all educational levels when people decide that they have arrived at the ultimate knowledge of God's ways. They are sure they know how God will answer. They have a spiritual superiority and intellectual certainty that borders on snobbery.

Regardless of the amount of your education, stay open to God's surprises. Let God be God! Don't be so closed that you know he has to answer a certain way. Remember that one of your favorite prayer promises says, "Call unto me, and I will answer thee, and shew thee great and mighty things, which thou knowest not" (Jer. 33:3).

Like Peter, God's answer stands knocking at many doors. It waits only for you to lift the latch, stop analyzing it to death, and humbly accept what God has sent.

The secret of spiritual satisfaction is willingness to accept the given. When God gives, you must be willing to accept the gift. You cannot demand another gift which you may prefer. Your problem begins when you say, "That's not what I wanted, Lord," or "I think I'll keep working at it until I come up with something better."

A real prayer is not so much to gain an object as it is to fill a need. If I pray for medicine it is because my body is sick. If my body is well when the medicine arrives, I have no need for the medication for which I prayed; and yet, my real prayer—for restored health—has been abundantly answered.

If I pray that God will perform a certain deed in order that I might believe, the real prayer is for faith, which very likely might come without the requested deed. So now I can be satisfied with my new faith in him.

Consider some possible answers which you have already received but haven't opened. You are praying for revival for your church, but it hasn't come. What happens in a genuine revival? For one thing, Christians get right with each other. Is there someone with whom you should be reconciled? Your answer is already given; when you make peace with your fellow Christians revival will come.

Also in revival, people repent of personal sins. Don't think about someone else, but only of yourself. Do you have unconfessed sin in your life? This is the reason for so many dead churches needing revival. Of course, a real revival will produce conversions. Is that an already given answer waiting to be opened? Certainly, for God is "not willing that any should perish, but that all should come to repentance" (2 Peter 3:9). How are people saved? Through our testimony and proclamation of the Good News. Every church office in the land already has enough names of unsaved people in the community to start a great revival in every church. What would happen in your church if you personally committed yourself to witnessing to definite lost people during a certain period of time? Your answer is waiting to be opened.

You may be unhappily married and praying for a way out. I have seen the miracle of love change cold dead marriages into exciting adventures. You may already be married to the best person on earth for you, if you could just find the real problem and work at it together.

You may be miserable in your job, but with a different attitude or different approach, you may change it into the dream situation. On the other hand, you may already know certain people who can open new doors. You may know the kind of preparation necessary to advance or change; if so, act on it and open your answer.

You may be needing wisdom to make an important decision, but you keep closing your ears to what God is trying to tell you. Many times I have had people come to me for counseling and they have complained that they have prayed and prayed but no answer has come. Often I have said, "But don't you see? When God leads you to someone for counseling, and new ideas for action are suggested, and a new perspective is given, you are sitting in the very midst of God's unfolding answer."

You may be praying for a great place of service, wondering why God is not using you, and in your own neighborhood someone is lonely, destitute, and helpless. I heard a story about D. L. Moody, who was approached by a woman who told him that God had called her to preach. He said, "Thank God, dear lady, that he has so blessed you. Do you have a family?" She replied, "Yes, I have a husband and ten children." The great evangelist roared, "Then, Madam, you are twice blessed. Not only has God called you to preach, he has already given you a congregation. Now, go home and feed your flock."

You may be praying for skill and talent to serve God, but you are not exercising the talent you already have. I believe for every person we see with outstanding ability that there are a thousand more who are equipped to do the same if they just would. I am reminded so often of those poignant lines of Oliver Wendell Holmes:

> *A few can touch the magic string,*
> *And noisy fame is proud to win them—*
> *Alas for those who never sing,*
> *But die with all their music in them.*

You may be complaining that God hasn't spoken to you lately. Be honest now. What did you do about the last thing he spoke to you about? I have learned that it is of little use asking God for some new message or some new gift if I haven't responded as he wanted me to when he last answered me. You ought not to expect God to give you something else until you have properly acted on his last revelation to you.

One of the saddest verses in the Bible is Jacob's comment upon awakening after the dream in which he saw God above the ladder. Jacob's words were, "Surely the

Lord is in this place; and I knew it not" (Gen. 28:16). How tragic to miss God in all the places you journey. How wasteful to spend a life without being conscious of the divine presence. How drab never to see the miracles in the margin, and the answers to prayer all around you. Elizabeth Barrett Browning said it so beautifully:

> *Earth's crammed with heaven*
> *And every common bush afire with God.*
> *But only he who sees takes off his shoes.*
> *All the rest sit around,*
> *And pick blackberries.*

I know personally from many long years of waiting that it can look like God will never answer our prayer. But sooner or later the most patient divine preparation must land us on the threshold of fulfillment; the invisible spiritual process must come to the point. God prepares slowly to face us suddenly! Our part is to be ready and to be willing to accept the answer when it comes. We must not forfeit the grand opportunity of being partners with God. We must not lose out on the joy of working in harmony with God, his world, and his plan for us. We must open the door and let the answer in. In *Julius Caesar*, Shakespeare reminded us:

> *There is a tide in the affairs of men,*
> *Which, taken at the flood, leads on*
>   *to fortune;*
> *Omitted, all the voyage of their life*
> *Is bound in shallows and miseries:*
> *And we must take the current*
>   *when it serves,*
> *Or lose our ventures.*

Now the last symbol is added to our diagram of harmonious praying. In the RFO circle of answers, the received answer is indicated by an arrow straight from God to you. The found answer is indicated by an arrow going out from you to search. And the opened answer is symbolized by an x within a smaller circle, indicating that God's answer is already here, waiting for you to claim it.

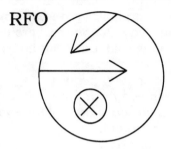

Try to get the completed symbol imprinted on your mind. When you pray, think consciously about the circle of your PSM: is this a primary prayer or a secondary prayer, and is it in harmony with the motive prayer for God's glory? Are your prayers in harmony with God as he is revealed to us? Do you pray in harmony with your own spiritual nature as the image of God, the child of God, and the handiwork of God? Do you pray in harmony with a world that is orderly, benevolent, and redemptive? Now, consider the RFO circle of God's answers. Are you willing to receive, find, and open the answers which God chooses to give you?

With a positive response to these questions, with a childlike faith, and a humble heart, your fellowship with God will begin to deepen and you will begin to get what you pray for!

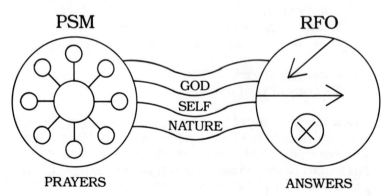